*Creating the Early Literacy Classroom*

# *Creating the Early Literacy Classroom*
## Activities for Using Technology to Empower Elementary Students

*Jean M. Casey*

**LIBRARIES**
U N L I M I T E D
A Member of the Greenwood Publishing Group

Westport, Connecticut • London

*To my mom, Marie, the best teacher*

ॐ

Libraries Unlimited
88 Post Road West,
Westport, CT 06881
1-800-225-5800
www.lu.com

**Library of Congress Cataloging-in-Publication Data**

Casey, Jean Marie.
    Creating the early literacy classroom : activities for using technology to empower elementary students / Jean M. Casey.
        p. cm.
Includes bibliographical references (p. ) and index.
ISBN 1-56308-712-X (pbk.)
1.Language arts (Elementary)--Computer-assisted instruction. 2. Computers and literacy. 3. English language--Computer-assisted instruction. I Title.

LB1576.7 .C38 2000
372.133'--dc21                                                      00-030426


05 04 03 EBA   10 9 8 7 6 5 4 3

# Contents

## List of Figures

*Photo by Kathi Kent.*

# *Foreword*

Each year, as I watch a new kindergarten class line up for the first time, I am touched by how excited they are. This is where they will learn to read and write, just like the big kids, just like grown-ups. They have already taught themselves to walk, and they have already taught themselves to talk, and they have mastered many wonderful skills. They have every hope and expectation that they will be successful here; to join what Dr. Casey calls "The Literacy Club."

Restructuring learning environments to empower young learners lies at the very heart of Dr. Casey's work. From the earliest days of her career, Dr. Casey's own work with children, and her accounts of research and case studies, reflect her commitment to literacy for all young learners. She chronicles the reading and writing successes of early learners when they are engaged in meaningful activities and given access to technology. Across the globe, her accounts show the connections between technology and early literacy. Anyone who works with young children knows that when children are denied access to this club we call literacy, they are denied their future. Dr. Casey presents the success stories that confirm the power of technology to empower children, to initiate them into "the club."

As we watch our world being transformed by technology, we find ourselves preparing children for a future we can only imagine. We know that they will need to become lifelong learners in an increasingly complex society. Without the ability to communicate, to collaborate, and to act as global citizens, they cannot hope to share in the promise of this new century. The success of our efforts to educate them will depend on our ability to provide learning environments that allow them to engage in these behaviors. Dr. Casey connects technology, writing, and children; communication, collaboration, and meaning; the need to know, the need to share, and the need to be heard. These connections provide the keys to unlocking the door to the literacy club for each and every child who stands in that line that first day of school.

**Toni Napier**
*Writing to Read Advisory Committee*
*Writing to Read Trainer*
*Technology Coordinator/Teacher*
*Archdiocese of Los Angeles, California*
*January 24, 2000*

# Part I

# Creating a Literacy Classroom

*Children who are excited about what they are doing tend to acquire the skills they need to do it well, even if the process takes a while. When interest is lacking, however, learning tends to be less permanent, less deeply rooted, less successful. Performance, we might say, is a by-product of motivation. (Kohn 1998)*

**"I can read!"** shouts five-year-old Timmy on the first day of kindergarten. This statement would have sounded like educational fiction in 1970 when I began teaching. When a kindergarten or first-grade child came to us then and asked, "Teacher, when will I learn to read?" we had to say, "Not until we teach you the 325 skills from our district Scope and Sequence Chart." The child would dejectedly return to his seat. But today in every classroom that has a good teacher and a talking word processor this can happen on the first day or first week of school for every child.

Are the children smarter? Are the teachers better? Maybe all of those things but the tools for communication are also much improved, and our knowledge about how children become literate is based on replicable global research studies. The new tools for communication in the classroom are the talking word processor, meaningful interactive phonics software and interactive CD-ROM books. These replace the pencil as the tools for students' daily writing, empowering them to express the ideas in their minds that they never before were able to write by using the pencil. Motivated by writing about their own interests and thoughts and validated by the professional-looking computer printout, students permanently learn the many skills they require to be literate. The key to these new tools is that they put the children in control of their own learning; and with this control comes empowerment and success when accompanied by the support and guidance of a teacher like you.

# Why Does the Computer Make Such a Difference for Early Writing and Reading?

To use a pencil well at age five requires a great deal of small motor coordination. Since eye-hand coordination is a developmental process that sometimes is not fully developed until they become seven or eight years old, many children have a great deal of difficulty with early attempts at writing. It also becomes a task equivalent to calligraphy when we require young learners to produce perfectly shaped letters on large lined paper—another task that leaves many of them frustrated and discouraged. When they can't get their ideas out on paper like the peers they see around them or the teacher who is writing on the board, they get discouraged. They make false judgments about their abilities and think they are poor students who are dumb or failures at the task of reading. Every teacher I have ever met has had one or more students who feel like this in their classroom. In the past they were assigned to the low reading group and given drill work, which further convinced many that school was not the place for them. The activities in this book will provide you with a new way to empower each of your students and help them become authors and readers. It is important that you are aware of the many factors that affect the "Learning to Read" process. Figure 1 is a list of those factors; keep them in mind as you assess and work with each of your students.

| PHYSICAL | 1. Vision: near point, far point, l-r tracking, eye movements: ABCs of vision difficulties, Snellen Test, tele-binocular, color blindness, visual discrimination, visual perception<br>2. Hearing: auditory perception, auditory discrimination, auditory memory, auditory acuity/Audiometer<br>3. Muscular coordination: large- and small-muscle control; hand-eye coordination<br>4. Consistent hand preference<br>5. General health, vigor; fatigue, diet<br>6. Speech<br>7. Neurological: endocrine imbalance |
|---|---|
| INTELLECTUAL | 1. Language development<br>2. Listening skills<br>3. Knowledge and concepts<br>4. Academic interest<br>5. First-hand experience |
| EMOTIONAL | 1. Self-concept<br>2. Birth order<br>3. Pressures from home, school, peers, community<br>4. Maturity, security, temper<br>5. Motivation<br>6. Attitude and outlook<br>7. Family support—personal problems (divorce, sibling rivalry) |
| SOCIAL | 1. Home background/Aspiration environment<br>2. Parental attitudes<br>3. Parental expectations<br>4. Teacher attitudes and expectations; other adults<br>5. Cultural difference<br>6. Sex and rank in family<br>7. Peer-group attitudes/ability to socialize, relate to peers |
| EDUCATIONAL | 1. Teacher<br>2. Poor instruction<br>3. Study habits<br>4. Inadequate vocabulary<br>5. Primary language preference<br>6. School administration<br>7. Class size<br>8. Methods/materials<br>9. Absences<br>10. Philosophy of school<br>11. Legislative factors<br>12. Risk-free supportive environment/technology support |
| OTHER CONSIDERATIONS | *Literacy Environment:* The classroom must be a place where literacy is modeled by the adults, where books, materials and writing tools are present and students are allowed to write and read daily. This environment needs to also be supported in the home, so close communication with parents is vital. This is a place for Authors and Readers—I am an author and a reader! A MEMBER OF THE LITERACY CLUB! |

*Now add your own factors: What other factors affected how you learned to read? Recall as much as you can and list important factors for you.*

**Figure 1. Factors That Affect Learning to Read**

# Why Should the Word Processor in Your Classroom Have Speech?

We learn through seeing, hearing, touching, moving. We all have our unique styles and strengths of learning. Many students profit from the auditory reinforcement they get when the computer reads back the words they have written. This auditory feature also helps with memory. It is an important feature to have in your classroom when you are trying to meet the needs of all your students.

You can read about research supporting the ideas that are the basis for the activities listed here in the revised edition of *Early Literacy: The Empowerment of Technology* (Casey 2000). *Creating the Early Literacy Classroom* will give you practical suggestions for designing your own writing, publishing room. Yours can be the best.

For the children who have not been successful in the reading method being taught, the procedure in schools often is to place them in special education. The numbers of occupants in these classes continue to grow. There's nothing wrong with our methods, so it must be the children, right? Wrong. We must abandon the attitude of blaming the child and instead focus on understanding that each human being is capable of learning. It is our job to create the best environment and empower students each to achieve their own potential. In special education, the search for devices to assist in communication has always been a concern and much of our educational technology has developed from that source.

According to the national definition of a balanced reading program, your classroom reading program must provide support for phonemic awareness, phonics instruction as well as comprehension skills and lots of writing and reading daily for all your students. (See Figure 2.)

A complete software program to accomplish many of these goals and provide appropriate support for each of your individual students would be to combine one of the available talking word processing programs with the best software available that presents phonemic awareness, vocabulary building, sentence building strategies and interactive CD-ROM books. Have a full classroom library, technology resources and you as the literacy model, and the writing, reading, speaking and publishing in your class will begin. This book suggests activities for using many types of programs. You can substitute other software programs that you find at the software clearinghouse; just keep in mind all the components listed here of a balanced reading program and try to make sure you have technology support for each area.

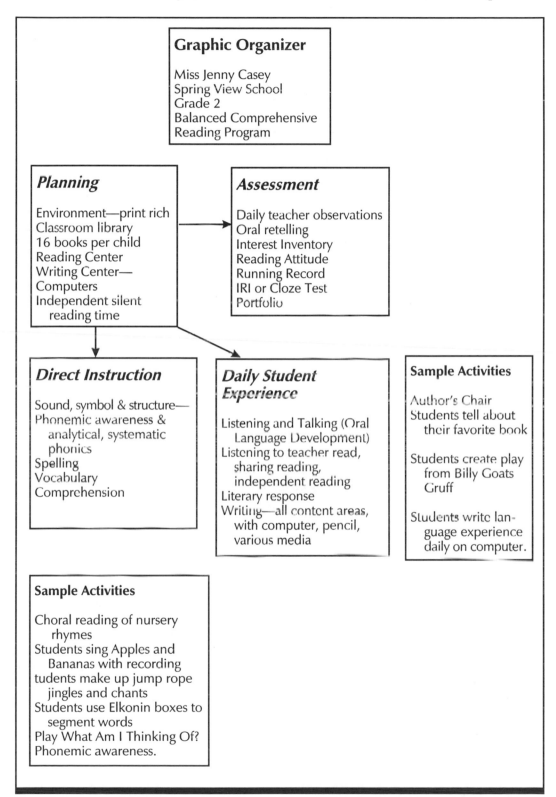

## Graphic Organizer

Miss Jenny Casey
Spring View School
Grade 2
Balanced Comprehensive
Reading Program

### Planning

Environment—print rich
Classroom library
16 books per child
Reading Center
Writing Center—
Computers
Independent silent
reading time

### Assessment

Daily teacher observations
Oral retelling
Interest Inventory
Reading Attitude
Running Record
IRI or Cloze Test
Portfolio

### Direct Instruction

Sound, symbol & structure—
Phonemic awareness &
analytical, systematic
phonics
Spelling
Vocabulary
Comprehension

### Daily Student Experience

Listening and Talking (Oral
Language Development)
Listening to teacher read,
sharing reading,
independent reading
Literary response
Writing—all content areas,
with computer, pencil,
various media

### Sample Activities

Author's Chair
Students tell about
their favorite book

Students create play
from Billy Goats
Gruff

Students write lan-
guage experience
daily on computer.

### Sample Activities

Choral reading of nursery
rhymes
Students sing Apples and
Bananas with recording
tudents make up jump rope
jingles and chants
Students use Elkonin boxes to
segment words
Play What Am I Thinking Of?
Phonemic awareness.

*Figure 2. Balanced Reading Program*

# Who Are These Computer Ideas For?

You need activities for English-language learners, you need activities for the gifted, you need activities for special education students, you need activities for slow readers; in fact, you need to be able to challenge every one of your students, right? Well, you have come to the right place. The ideas and activities presented in this book are designed just for the children you serve. They are open-ended and meaningful. They will motivate each of your students. The topics are based on engaging the students' interest and their need to know. Most important, they each respond at their own ability level.

Your most important role is to be supportive and empowering. You can do this in the following ways:

1. You accept all your students as learning, caring human beings whom you know can be successful.

2. You offer encouragement and excitement about each day's learning.

3. You model your own personal writing in each area as inspiration for your students to create their own writings.

4. You show joy in reading their work and your keen assessment of the skills they have acquired and those you find you must guide them in accomplishing.

5. You give your students daily access to the talking word processor and problem-solving software so that they can use these sophisticated tools to enhance their learning.

6. You avoid the use of programmed instructional learning system drill-type computer materials or games that confound the learner by confusing the learning.

When we teach children through our own disciplined and caring actions in the world, we take an authentic stance. We use the most basic and fundamental principle of teaching: our actions speak louder than our words. It is then that children say, "I see you, I see everything." (Charney 1992)

Review all software carefully. I just reviewed a software program purporting to teach students verbs; I found it focused more on a monkey climbing a tree and then having the student choose how he would dive in the water than on helping students understand sentence building. These types of programs are a waste of your students' time. When you use the talking word processor and students write what they think daily, they are using verbs and your coaching helps them refine these skills. Steer clear of poor software and isolated drill programs.

## ❧ Benefits of Using a Computer with Talking Word Processor in Your Classroom for Children to Write Daily ❧

1.  It can help children hear and understand the sound patterns of English as they use the talking word processor to read, speak and write.

2.  It motivates children to write. Writing becomes an interactive and dynamic form of expression when children can hear their text immediately spoken back to them. Text-to-speech output can be controlled by the children, allowing them to hear their text as often as necessary. This takes away the child's negative experience of having to repeatedly ask for a teacher's help to make the program work or to understand the words on the screen.

3.  It allows children to read and write English before they have mastered the mechanics of literacy such as letter names and sight vocabulary. They do not get "stuck" so easily. If they have trouble reading a word, they can direct the computer to say the word and act as a decoder.

4.  Speech coupled with visual display helps focus the children's attention on the language activity.

5.  It provides the necessary auditory component in the learning environment. The children can hear, see and touch information about written language.

6.  It increases creativity and skill in written self-expression as children hear and critique their own written work. With the speech component, children, even at a very young age, can become active creative writers.

7.  It allows even the young child to be an autonomous learner able to master program operation through spoken instructions and help messages.

8.  It allows a high degree of personalization by incorporating spoken reinforcement messages customized for each individual child.

9.  It can be a voice for children who have difficulty speaking. Because children with language disabilities can learn to write sentences before they speak them, their oral language skills are improved by seeing the text and hearing it spoken.

10. It provides audio validation for menu selections and program operation for visually impaired users.

11. It makes it possible for children to change word pronunciation and make the connection between how words sound in contrast to their English spelling.

English, despite its complexity, can be reduced to about 50 discreet sounds, called *phonemes*. Text-to-speech systems are designed to operate by breaking text into phonetic building blocks and then pronouncing those building blocks in units that more or less resemble words.

Today the technology is available for students to record their own names, thoughts and experiences on a keyboard. This makes the writing process much easier for them. They now can hear the words they have created read by the computer, see them on the screen, read with the computer and print out a professional-looking copy of what they have written. I call this method *language processing* because the students are now able to write their own language experiences, thoughts and ideas without having someone else take dictation and write for them. This early intervention of daily language processing for each student is opening the door to literacy for all.

# How Do Children Do Language Processing?

The computer, when used as a writing tool, offers success to all learners. After years of observing young children at the keyboard, I have recorded the process by which they achieve literacy when using the microcomputer as their learning tool.

1.  **Exploration**. Initially students explore the keyboard and type random letters. This exploration is an essential learning stage. As they type a key, they see it, hear it and are actively involved in the process of teaching the letters to themselves. (Alphabet recognition has been shown to be an indicator of reading success.)

2.  **Encoding and copying known words**. Next the students type their name and words familiar to them like Mom, Dad, Ruff, etc. They also look around their environment for print and type that print into the computer and hear it spoken and see its form; they continually search for meaning and patterns in the letters and words they create on the screen.

3.  **Writing explosion**. Finally students begin to put their own thoughts together with all these words. The explosion of literacy from one sentence on the screen to long stories occurs very rapidly.

At this stage, the learners need to hear the teacher read many and varied examples of good literature. This listening acquisition of authors' styles and content serves as a fount of ideas for them to assimilate, adapt and use in the creation of their own individual stories. The final proof of their membership in the literacy club is the professional-looking computer-printed copy of their own language, now a real book or story.

This is the proof that they are indeed authors and literate people. The empowerment that occurs to every beginner through this approach warrants its use. In an environment free of risk and with a teacher who facilitates the language development, language processing occurs in a natural manner much akin to the acquisition of speech.

Some effective software programs that I have found in working with K-5 students for this purpose are KidWorks Deluxe and KidPhonics, both available from Knowledge Adventure (1999b, a) and the Living Books Series from Broderbund. KidPhonics includes music and song lyrics and allows the child to notice sounds in meaningful context. It is exactly what teachers have been asking for, and does a good job helping students gain phonemic awareness and knowledge of letter sounds. The Ultimate Writing and Creativity Center by the Learning Company (1998) is another excellent choice, especially for middle grades and above. KidPix (Learning Company, 1999) is another fine program that has the talking word processor in both English and Spanish. This is a great asset in bilingual classes for English learners.

With the rapid technology explosion, newer, better products are always on the horizon and as an educator you must continually review new software products that accomplish the goals of your classroom. The place to begin when integrating technology in the classroom is to determine the goals you wish to accomplish; then find the software that achieves those goals and choose the hardware that will run those programs. Refer to the California Instructional Technology Clearinghouse, http://www.clearinghouse.k12.ca.us, for the latest reviews of software (Lathrop 1995). Another resource for you to check is the Children's Software Revue at http://www.childrenssoftware.com or Educational Software Institute at http://www.edsoft.com.

I cannot stress enough to you the importance of your careful preview and selection of software. Always ask yourself, "Is the student in control of his or her learning and what is the objective of this program? How will the student benefit?" In *The Promise and the Threat of Microcomputers in Language Education*, Frank Smith said, "If computers are just used for drill and kill we would be better off without them" (Smith 1984). The promise or hope of technology in the literacy classroom is realized when it is used as a tool to empower the student to read and write.

As you work with children in your classroom, you will observe how computers now allow children and adults to move easily between text and graphics. Most children will use mixes of graphic forms and keyboard letters from early preschool years into first grade. They profit greatly from the ease of use of the computer. First they type random letters and enjoy listening to the sounds made by the computer. They find some strings of letters and words hilarious and often laugh out loud at the sounds they have created. When they hear the computer mispronounce a word, they find it amusing, but as they become more fluent, they begin to change their spelling so the computer will say the words they want it to say.

You will find children adapt easily to computer writing. They start with hunt and peck, which helps them attend to alphabet recognition and also develop the strategies they need to write. They definitely do not need touch typing to begin to write. When they begin writing daily you need to introduce the keyboard and home keys: see Figure 3 that we used with kindergarten and first graders in the classroom. With a simple little story we explained that the pinky finger stays on *a* but visits the neighbor keys *q* and *z* as well. This kind of in-class activity along with paper keyboards is the place to start. Then you need to choose a touch typing program like the typing program included in the Waterford Early Reading Series or some of the others you find in the Clearinghouse reviews, and always look for a desirable or exemplary rating on the software.

You will get to know your students and the problems they are facing in their daily lives and how they are dealing with those problems. In one class I worked with, there was an especially poignant story written by a first-grade girl that showed how a child, through her writing, can use a combination of make-believe and real-world happenings to work out her own personal feelings. Although this little girl chose a fictitious name and culture for the little girl she wrote about, the problem in the story was her own. Her mom was pregnant but didn't tell her; in fact, the mom thought her daughter didn't know what the word *pregnant* meant (children can be much wiser than we give them credit for!). The child was feeling excluded and worried about sharing the attention of the adults with a new baby. See Figure 4. A teacher reading this kind of story can use discussion and literature such as *Peter's Chair* by Ezra Keats (Keats 1998) to help the child work through her fears of a new baby in the family. Without this new tool that allows children to write what is on their minds every day, the teacher could not provide this type of meaningful learning.

Printing out children's daily writing is another important feature of using technology. Children need to be given the opportunity to print out their pieces daily, and then share them in class and at home with parents and other family members. Collecting published versions of children's stories into classroom books or encouraging them to write their own books will put more interest and energy into their writing. Daniel, a five-year-old Hispanic student, was focused and compelled to write as he wrote his own Spanish version of Disney's *Lion King* and set it to music for his whole class of five-year-olds to enjoy. Steven Spielberg, watch out—Daniel is creating marvelous productions too!

*Text continues on page 15.*

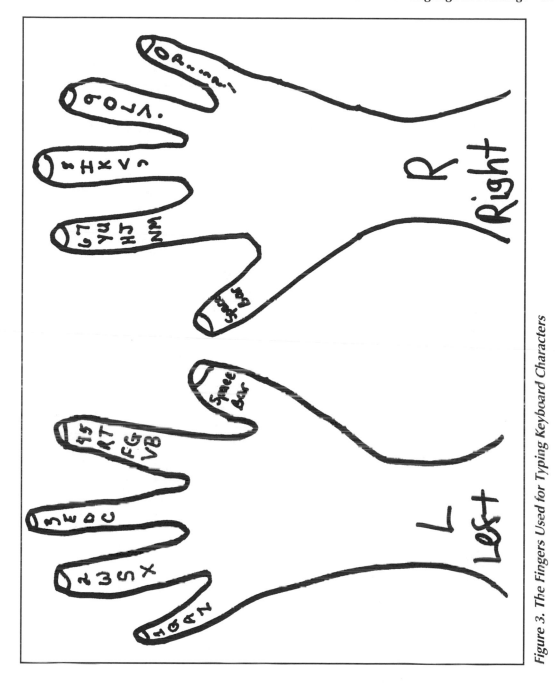

*Figure 3. The Fingers Used for Typing Keyboard Characters*

Sarah

The    LonLy Indin    Girl
Once upon        a time there was   a
     beutiful but lonly
     Indin girl.Her nam e was Tiffn'y

She had lots of pets but, she
did'nt have any friends.

She was nine years old. Then   one Brit
beutiful day her mother said was I'm
going   to the hosbitle   tomorrw Ok
ok she said.

*Figure 4. The LonLy Indin Girl Story*

The next day Tiffiny asked her mother why she was going to the hosbitle? All her mother ansered was I haveto go there because I have a job there .

That was all she said then she left. But a while later her mother came back with a little baby. It was a girl.

*Figure 4 continues on page 14.*

Tiffiny   thoght about the bab ywhen she could
play with her.She                 was nt lonly
INEMORE.


THE END   ?!

# What Do You Need to Turn Your Classroom into a Publishing Center?

> *I have seen children in "Special Ed." classes use the computer militantly as to assert their real identity against School's classification of them as incompetent. (Papert 1993)*

The first ingredient is your own enthusiasm and knowledge that having this empowering tool in your classroom will greatly foster the literacy development of your students, especially those who might fail with other approaches. Next you need the support of your administrator, school district and parents of your students. They must all understand that the goal of your program is to use technology as a problem-solving tool to empower your students' literacy development. They must understand that you will not be using it as a game machine, or drill and kill on computer, or CAI delivery system that treats the student like a drone on the keyboard. You need to bring them together and share the research and benefits for students found in the revised edition of *Early Literacy: The Empowerment of Technology* (Casey 2000).

Once you have heightened awareness and established need, then you are ready to ask for six networked computers in your classroom, with one hooked up to a projection monitor for your group language experience lessons.

Years of research have shown that the greatest benefit of using technology in the classroom comes when it is used as a writing tool or problem-solving tool. With the learner in control, the talking word processor is a sophisticated pencil that allows students who previously failed in pencil-writing tasks to be successful writers. The immediate success provided in the writing task enhances the learners' self-concept and allows them to feel like an author from the first day of school.

Your classroom should be filled with meaningful print, especially the daily writings of your students. This enriched literacy environment enables students to develop understandings about reading and writing so that they learn in a meaningful way. Students can write their own lyrics to songs that they already are familiar with. See Figure 5 for a Halloween song written by a five-year-old to the tune of "Frere Jacques." For example, pick a song like "Grandma's Featherbed" and play the cassette tape for your students. Then give them each a copy of the lyrics that you have printed out from your computer. Suggest to the children that they each write out things that they remember from their grandma's house. They can put their new lyrics to the melody and share their new song with the group. The simultaneous visual and auditory processing of text has been shown to be very beneficial to developing readers (Chomsky 1978). The word processor is a perfect companion to your literature program. Children's reading skills grow from their daily re-reading of their own writing as well as from daily reading of literature books and the writings of their peers. Many children really like to create their own versions of stories from books, and it is not unusual to see them bring a book to the computer to assure that they use a conventional spelling or idea.

*A note about phonemic spelling:* The spelling used in the sample stories included provide you with an excellent assessment of a child's knowledge of sound-symbol correspondences and phonics generalizations. Just like approximation in speech occurs naturally in language acquisition, children use their phonemic knowledge to approximate spelling at early developmental levels. Observations of young children show that they use their knowledge of phonology to invent spellings. In the first four or five years of writing, children move from phonemic to book spelling. This learning happens through reading and writing experiences; the daily writing on the computer will greatly foster this development.

Holli

**Figure 5. Holli's Halloween Song**

You and your students together will come up with many ideas for them to write on the computer and read what they have written. This method provides the most meaningful and comprehensible input that a student needs for beginning reading and writing. Their final products prove that they are authors; sharing one another's writings proves they are readers.

Throughout the year by using these activities, you will be building a classroom library with books authored by your students. All the activities require students to write something. After they have written their piece, they will work with a partner on editing their work for publication. You need to have a team of students responsible for binding everyone's work into a class book. This team can be changed throughout the year to give everyone the chance to participate and to learn how to take a piece of writing from the first draft to a final published version.

Enjoy these activities as they help you create the best, most meaningful classroom library you have ever had. As an added bonus along the way, you will get to know each of your students better through their daily writings. Your pleasure will be seeing their growth and enjoying the many creative stories they will write.

LET'S GET STARTED TODAY!

### Special Needs

Leave no one out. If you have mainstreamed special-needs students, look for adaptive devices and appropriate software to empower them. Visit the Closing the Gap website at http://closingthegap.com/ to find special software, enlarged or Braille text, special speech synthesizers, voice-entry systems, touch screens, adaptive firmware card, alternate keyboards, and headpointers, among others.

# Part II

# *Activities for the K-8 Classroom*

**All the activities** in this book can be scaled up or down to meet the needs of your students. You should select the most interesting and appropriate ones for your students. Feel free to pick and choose and vary the sequence; you will find that some of them lend themselves to many different writing pieces. The key to good teaching is to match the activity to the interest and needs of your students and not the other way around, prescribing to students whether they need the activity or not!

*Writing Across the Curriculum.* These activities can be adapted for writing across the curriculum, so change topics to meet the units and subjects that you are teaching but incorporate the creative writing and reporting ideas that you will find in this book. All the activities in this book can be adapted to be used in the classroom with one or more computers, in the Library Media Center with multiple computers and in a computer lab.

*What if I have only one computer in my classroom?*

> ➤ *If this is the case, Activities 1–3 contain ideas to support your literacy program in the one-computer classroom.*

## ✎1. Teacher Uses of One Computer

**Procedure:** Write the daily messages or a story for your students that you wish to write for them so that they see you as an author and a reader.

Write frequent newsletters and parent notes to keep parents as your constant partners in supporting their child's literacy. E-mail other staff members and parents.

E-mail educators worldwide and broaden your knowledge about how children learn; link up with colleagues who can help you problem solve issues in your classroom. There's no need to feel isolated ever again in your class. As you can see, the word processor with speech encourages a wide range of literacy activities.

## ✎2. Group Language Experience Story

**Procedure:** Wheel the computer to the front of the class using either a projection monitor or large-screen TV monitor. Gather the children around the front of the computer so all can see and participate.

Pick a topic. Let students choose a recent event at school or in their community (e.g., The Fourth of July Parade in our town) and talk about it. You will type the sentences they contribute on the computer, and they will see their language validated on the big screen. For example, have a volunteer give a sentence, then type exactly what the child says: "John says he marched in the parade with his Cub Scout Troop." Let the computer read John's sentence back to the class, ask John if that is correct and then let him read his sentence along with the computer. Get a sentence from each child using the same procedure.

When the story is complete, have the group decide on an appropriate title for the story and print out a copy for each child and have a choral or whole-class reading of the entire story along with the computer. Have each child skim and scan the story to find his name and circle it. You can also do a group phonics or vocabulary lesson by highlighting beginning letters, onsets and rhymes, word endings and interesting descriptive words. Choose these based on the needs you know your students have from their daily writings.

This type of group language experience activity integrates the knowledge for the students. It helps them learn that:

- Their language is important and meaningful.

- What they can say can be written; what they can write can be read.

- They are all authors of this group story that they can read. (Keep these stories bound in a notebook titled "Our Class Stories.")

- They can recognize their names and many words they already know.

- Words are made up of letters that we represent in speech with sounds.

The next most important use of your one computer with speech is to try and give daily access for writing to as many students as possible but particularly:

- Those who have difficulty writing anything with a pencil.

- Those who exhibit signs of dyslexia (word reversals or confusions) or A.D.D. (attention deficit disorder).

- Gifted students who finish the normal assignment quickly and are motivated to write a long story.

Schedule students for fifteen minutes daily to each have writing time at your computer and have it occupied all day long, every day.

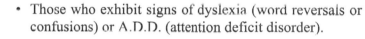

## ❧ 3. More Group Language Experience

**Procedure:** The teacher or a student types the story into the word processor; the class sees the story on the large screen and reads it as it is typed. The group edits the story, prints out copies and the group uses the story as a shared choral reading experience. Have students all contribute to this story about what has been happening in your classroom.

Use this as an opportunity for collaboration but, also an opportunity to model phonics, sentence structure, grammar and punctuation and discuss editing. Let the computer read the completed story to the class and listen for places that need change or editing.

(This is a great strength of the talking word processor; often when we re-read our own writing we miss mistakes but hearing it read back to us we catch the errors and can self-correct.) Editing should be taught from kindergarten on up through all the grades; as children re-read and hear the computer read what they have written on the computer, it becomes very natural to edit their work. Print out the edited copy for each student and do a shared reading exercise, with choral reading or with students reading the part of the story they contributed. Give them time and the freedom to create the words they choose and listen to it read by the computer as many times as they want.

## ✌4. *Writing in Pairs or Small Groups*

**Procedure:** Let students work in pairs or small groups and collaborate on stories; they can take turns dictating and typing. The computer needs to be in use all day to give you the maximum integration in your curriculum and student empowerment. Let students choose partners based on interest in writing a specific type of story. Have a writer's contest where you turn in these story collaborations and have them compete for a prize, or select the best ones to be in the class newsletter or on a special bulletin board. This kind of activity encourages cooperative learning and teamwork, a skill essential in today's workplaces.

## ✌5. *Picture Books*

**Procedure:** There are many beautiful Caldecott Medal award winning books for illustration. Students today are very visual learners, being tuned in to so much video since infancy. Here's a way to capture their interest in visuals, expand their sense of art and develop their imaginative language. Bring in the book *Tuesday* by David Wiesner (Wiesner 1999). Show your students the beautiful artistic work in this book—pictures that create a mood and mystery. Challenge them to look at the illustrations and think of a story to go with the setting. They can type this story on the computer and then share it with the group. Talk to them about imagination and how important it is that we take time to dream and imagine.

## ❧ 6. Especially for Gifted Students

Often your gifted students come to you reading already. John Goodlad, a well-known educator and author, described his early education in an interview. He had been reading quite a bit before he went to school. By the time he was halfway through the first grade, he would come home and read the primer. He had it memorized, so he quit reading. The teachers at the time used phonetic approaches to reading, which he found to be absolutely silly. So he would go to the chalkboard, and find a word he knew he could read and be told to break it down into these little pieces. Having a rebellious nature at times, he rebelled against reading as it was being taught. At the end of the year, his parents were told he would not be promoted. His father would not allow that and he went on the next year to flourish in a classroom that valued his intelligence (Tell 1999).

There is a danger today with political and state dictates to teach isolated analytical phonics to students whether they need it or not. This practice is turning off students who are potential gifted leaders of tomorrow, as John Goodlad is today. We cannot allow this to happen to our gifted students, who are often insulted, bored or neglected in our classrooms. They are one of our greatest resources for the future. As a teacher you must recognize their intelligence and the skills they have already achieved. In a writing, publishing classroom you can inspire them to write. Encouraging them to do research and learn at the exceptionally high level of their ability will challenge them. They need never be bored, turned-off or disheartened in your room, but rather they can create and write at a level to inspire everyone.

**Procedure:** Read the *The Hobbit* by J. R. R. Tolkien (Tolkien 1977) to the students and challenge them to create their own world like the one that Tolkien created. This can be a long-term project with them expanding on the story during their daily writing. Perhaps they have another author that they really like; encourage them to write a story in that style or genre.

## ❧ 7. Language Processing/Writing by Myself

**Procedure:** Language processing is writing one's own thoughts, ideas and stories directly on a computer and then editing them by listening to the computer read them back, or reading along with the computer.

## Cardinal Rule for Your Classroom

*Let the students create their story and type it directly into the computer by themselves. Do not have them write it out first and then copy it on the computer. That's a good way to make them dislike the computer after struggling with their pencil skills.*

Creating an atmosphere where storytelling flourishes is one step in the process of learning to be storywriters. Children also need to learn how to organize and focus their stories so that a reader can make sense of them. It is your job as a teacher to help them with this. In Activity 1 you modeled writing a group language processing story. From now on you want your students to compose the story themselves. In the beginning we might have the student dictate the story to us and write it for them, but we do not want to continue doing this for it takes the control of the storytelling away from the child; it requires the mediation of an adult scribe and interpreter. This loss of control is a high price to pay for getting the story into print (Karelitz 1993).

## ✎8. More Individual Language Processing

**Purpose:** Self-expression, empowerment as a writer, noticing word forms, receiving multimodal feedback as words are read back, experimenting with letters, words, phrases.

**Procedure:** Have students begin a new file or story. Encourage them to type their names, names of people in their families, pets, letters of the alphabet they know or want to learn, and any words they see in the room that they would like to learn. Give them time and the freedom to create the words they choose and listen to it read by the computer as many times as they want. Allow children to print out their story. If time allows, encourage them to illustrate their story either on the computer or by hand. See Figure 6.

> *Note: This first stage of writing is very important. You need to be the encourager, listener and facilitator to help develop a student's expanded language and writing. Praise the student's writing and then ask questions such as, "What color is your dog?" "Write more about him."*

Let at-risk learners or students in scribble stage write mock letters or play with language forms. Encourage them to start with the graphics part of your writing program and draw a picture and then talk about their picture. Encourage them to type a phrase, caption or sentence under their pictures, print out, read it to others in the

what I love
I love the cumputterlab. I love
wrighting tiping. I love storys.
I love cumputteers. I love ever
thing.

Lesley

*Figure 6. What I Love Story*

class and proudly take it home to read to their families. Keep the daily language experience lessons in a portfolio. After you have a large selection, let students select their favorite, revisit it on the computer for simple editing and print out and illustrate it: "My Book About Me."

## 9. A Progressive Story

**Procedure:** This activity is a lot of fun, and it gets cooperative learning going amongst your students.

Select someone to be the first author, decide with the class what kind of story you will be writing together: a fairy tale, mystery, adventure, science fiction, fantasy, funny story, true-life story, animal story, etc. Give your students a list of first lines for each kind of story such as:

| | |
|---|---|
| Once upon a time | for the fairy tale |
| It was a dark and story night | for the mystery |
| We started to climb the mountain | for the adventure |
| The alien had three green eyes | for the science fiction |
| The giant and the little people all appeared | for the fantasy |
| He looked like a chocolate puppy covered with mud | for the funny story |
| I had a very exciting day yesterday | for the true-life story |

The first author goes to the computer and writes the first part of the story. Allow about ten minutes per student to write their part. When they are finished, they come back to the group and tap someone on the shoulder who goes and reads or listens to the computer read what has been written so far. This student writes the next part of the story.

After all students in a group or the class have contributed to the story, play the story on the projection monitor for the whole class to enjoy. Print out copies for the whole class to do a choral reading together, and, of course, keep a bound copy of this story in your class library.

## ✎ 10. English Language Development—Using the Computer to Help Develop English Skills

Learners are motivated to use language when they have:

*1. An authentic reason to communicate.* The talking word processor empowers them to communicate easily with others in print, with penpals online and working collaboratively in small groups.

*2. Comprehensible input.* Language acquisition occurs when learners understand the messages. Multisensory input such as visuals, graphic organizers and drawing all aid comprehension. The software program KidWorks Deluxe provides the child with this environment. Best of all, each child is in control of her learning. By selecting a sticker picture, they see the word, hear the word and can insert it in their stories. Research with second-language learners has proven that this multisensory approach to language learning is very effective (Casey 2000).

**Procedure:** Using KidWorks Deluxe, have students choose sticker graphics to place in their stories that cover a large range of animals, food, clothing and words in the children's environment. Let the students copy words they see in the room and listen to the words read by the computer. They now can decode any word in their environment independently; this is a fantastic tool for learning vocabulary.

## ✎ 11. Letter Recognition—Names and Shapes of Letters

# ABCDEFGHIJkLMNOPQ
# rstuvwxyz

**Procedure:** Sing the ABC song with your class and introduce one of the many available ABC books such as Chris Van Allsburg's *The Z Was Zapped* (Van Allsburg 1987) or Graeme Base's *Animalia* (Base 1983).

Model a lesson for your group on your computer and project it on a screen for the entire class. Type the ABCs slowly on the screen, asking the class to say them with you. Then sing the ABC song, pointing to the letters on the screen, and let the computer say the letters. Print out the letters and give each child a copy to hold while you sing the ABC song together.

Have the students locate the letter their name begins with. Have them pick a partner and take turns pointing to a letter for the partner to identify. When the partnership thinks they know all the letters, they can come up and recite them to the class.

Now let your students work at the computer to locate the letters they are learning. Show them how the CAPS LOCK key works and encourage them to try and write the entire alphabet with a space between each letter in CAPITAL LETTERS, then let the computer read them back.

Have them release the caps lock and type all the ABCs in lowercase letters, and listen to the computer read them back.

Remember that students need time at the computer just for exploration of letters, to hear how they sound, to write words they know or see in their environment. Give them this opportunity daily. Let them print out what they have created and read it to three people in the room; they can illustrate it if they like.

> *Important note: Always have students listen to the computer read what they wrote, read it with the computer, print it out, and then read it to at least three people in class. Students must be in control of their learning; this is the place for you to be extremely flexible yet very observant. You must be able to judge when a child is ready to move to the next step and give the child the appropriate instruction and encouragement to reach that step.*

You already know about the California Instructional Technology Clearinghouse—this is a Web address to mark as a favorite place on your browser and visit frequently when selecting software programs for your class. Another software program rated exemplary by the software clearinghouse is ABC Animals by AGC Educational Media; this program presents the alphabet in song. The students learn sound/letter correspondence, say the letter, sing the sound of the letter, and see the letter flash on the screen. It uses captivating graphics to present words beginning with each letter (AGC Educational Media 1999). The Waterford Early Reading Program also does an outstanding job at teaching alphabet recognition (Waterford Institute, 1990).

## 12. Letter Play

**Procedure:** Show students how to choose different fonts, then let them pick the letters that start their name or a letter they would like to learn and write it in as many styles as they can. Then using the stickers graphic function in KidWorks Deluxe, have them find as many sticker pictures as they can that begin with the letter they are using and place them in their story. For example, if they chose the letter D, they can print out a D book. See Figure 7.

*Figure 7. Danielle's D Book*

## 13. My Name

**Procedure:** Using your name as an example, show the children all the ways you can write your name on the computer and hear it read back to you. Suggest they write their names in as many ways as they can think of and then print it out; they might want to do this with other family members' names as well. Show them how to copy it and paste it again and again on their screen. Watch their delight as the computer reads their names over and over again.

Here's what Katie did!

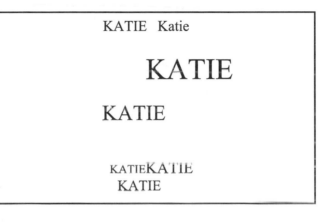

## 14. Sight Words or Words in the Environment

**Procedure:** Encourage the students to copy any words they want to learn from the dictionary or in their reading materials on the word processor and let the computer read them back to them. Provide the students with the following list of thirty-six most common words. (Have a chart of these words near the computers so they can copy and listen to these words.)

Encourage the children to type these words on the computer and then listen to the computer read them as often as they like. Next they should try reading the words along with the computer. When they feel ready, they can test themselves by reading the words on the computer screen out loud to the teacher or a peer. They can also record their reading of the words on KidWorks Deluxe and check to see if they have them all correct. You can select other vocabulary word lists or the one hundred most frequently used sight words or let students choose their own words from dictionaries to type and listen to on the computer. This is a fantastic tool for all children, especially English learners, to learn new vocabulary.

## ❧ *36 Most Common Words* ❧

| | | | | | |
|---|---|---|---|---|---|
| the | and | to | a | I | said |
| you | in | it | of | he | was |
| is | on | that | she | for | can |
| they | his | all | what | we | will |
| not | little | with | my | do | but |
| are | at | up | her | have | out |

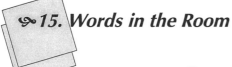

## ❧ 15. *Words in the Room*

**Procedure:** Have the student write the names of things they see in the room (e.g., clock), people they see in the room, their favorite foods, toys, etc. Have the students look around the room and find words and then type the words into their computer file and try to predict what the word is and then have the computer speak it. The next time have them read it along with the computer. Challenge them to try and find as many words as they can in the room, or write as many words as they think they know. Remember that after they print out their work, they are to read it to at least three people in class.

## ✎ 16. Number Play

**Procedure:** Letters are not the only thing the talking computer can help students learn. Numbers work as well. Students can type any numbers they wish on the computer, such as

# 1 2 3 4 5 6 7 8 9 0

The computer will then read the numbers, and the students can write the words for each number: one, two, three, four, five, six, seven, eight, nine, zero. Introduce numbers to your students and then tell them to count as high as they can on the computer by writing the number and then a space and then having the computer read their numbers back to them.

## ✎ 17. Place Value

**Procedure:** Demonstrate to your students, using your computer and KidWorks, how you can write a number like 2,000 and the computer will read it correctly. Tell them to write some numbers and try to read them correctly and then have the computer read them and see if they were right. They can work in pairs with one student writing the number and the other student reading it. They can use the computer speech to see who read it correctly. This is a great way to teach place value. They can write large numbers like 897,543 and the computer will read it accurately. This helps them learn to read large numbers up to the millions. Give your students an opportunity to learn about numbers in this way and then print out their work for a class book, "About Numbers."

## ✎ 18. Onset and Rimes

**Procedure:** Put a list of word families on the board. Encourage students to select one family, and by substituting beginning letters, make as many words as they can think of with this family and then read the words with the computer. They can delete any that do not make words that they recognize.

The next step is to try and write simple poems or use the rhyming words to make a sentence such as:

## The black back pack is on my stack, said Jack.

Students will have lots of fun having the computer read these rhyming sentences they have created. Display the following list of 37 Rimes and tell the students to pick a word family and write a poem

## ❧ *The 37 Rimes and Common Words Using Them* ❧

| Rime | Words |
|------|-------|
| -ack | black, pack, quack, stack |
| -ail | mail, nail, sail, tail |
| -ain | brain, chain, plain, rain |
| -ake | cake, shake, take, wake |
| -ale | male, sale, tale, whale |
| -ame | came, flame, game, name |
| -an | can, man, pan, than |
| -ank | bank, drank, sank, thank |
| -ap | cap, clap, map, slap |
| -ash | cash, dash, flash, trash |
| -at | bat, cat, rat, that |
| -ate | gate, hate, late, plate |
| -aw | claw, draw, jaw, saw |
| -ay | day, play, say, way |
| -eat | beat, heat, meat, wheat |
| -ell | bell, sell, shell, well |
| -est | best, chest, nest, west |
| -ice | ice, mice, nice, rice |
| -ick | brick, pick, sick, thick |
| -ide | bride, hide, ride, side |
| -ight | bright, fight, light, might |
| -ill | fill, hill, kill, will |
| -in | chin, grin, pin, win |
| -ine | fine, line, mine, nine |
| -ing | king, sing, thing, wing |
| -ink | pink, sink, think, wink |
| -ip | drip, hip, lip, ship |
| -ir | fir, sir, stir |
| -ock | block, clock, knock, sock |
| -oke | choke, joke, poke, woke |
| -op | chop, drop, hop, shop |
| -ore | chore, more, shore, store |
| -or | for, or |
| -uck | duck, luck, suck, truck |
| -ug | bug, drug, hug, rug |
| -ump | bump, dump, hump, lump |
| -unk | bunk, dunk, junk, sunk |

with that. Learning these word families will help them recognize words from these groups. Allowing them the choice in selecting words and creating their own writing also enhances the learning.

## 19. Word Walls

Word walls are a good way to highlight students' attention to words they are reading in content area books or studying in thematic units. Students and the teacher choose words to write on word walls, which are large sheets of paper hanging in the classroom.

**Procedure:** Decide on a unit of instruction or topic you are teaching. Develop a word wall in your classroom for a vocabulary lesson, encourage children to type those words on the computer, listen to the computer read them and then read them along with the computer.

When they feel they know the words well, they can print them out and draw a graphic to go with the words and help them remember them. This is a very effective way to learn new vocabulary.

### ❧ Word Wall About Our Favorite Foods ❧

| | | | | |
|---|---|---|---|---|
| Spaghetti | Pizza | Hot Dogs | Hamburgers | Carrots |
| Macaroni | Pot Pies | Sandwiches | French Fries | Lettuce |

## 20. Compound Word Fun

**Procedure:** Use your computer and big screen to show your students how you create compound words. On the screen create some words like *blockbuster* or a meaningful print word they would recognize. Talk about how we make compound words and then give each child one of the compound word lists to take to the computer with them.

Duplicate the word lists included here and challenge students to make up as many compound words as they can. After they make up each word, they should listen to it to see if it makes sense. When they get their final list, they should listen to the computer read the list and then read along with the computer. Finally have them print out their list and exchange it with a peer and try to see if they can read one another's word lists. Every time they read someone's entire list correctly, they get to sign their name on the back of it. The person whose name appears on the back of the most lists is the winner and gets to be listed as the word wizard for the week on the board.

---

### ❧ *Compound Word Lists* ❧

| | |
|---|---|
| any | one |
| some | how |
| base | shine |
| foot | body |
| sun | ball |
| day | plane |
| night | side |
| no | day |
| air | thing |
| out | quake |
| in | time |
| up | how |
| every | light |
| earth | where |

---

## ❧ 21. Word Play and Pattern Stories

**Procedure:** Read books full of word play to your students such as the Amelia Bedelia books (Parish 1992) or *Sheep in a Jeep* by Nancy Shaw (Shaw 1988). Encourage your students to think of words that rhyme and silly words and write them in their stories. *Rosie's Walk* by Pat Hutchins (Hutchins 1983) is a pattern story. After hearing one of these stories, Mechelle wrote her own pattern story. See Figure 8.

Mechelle

I see a cat in a tree.
I see a dog in a tree.
I see a fish in a tree.
I see a pig in a tree.
I see a sun in a tree.
I see a bed in a tree.
I see a leg in a tree.
I see a man in a tree.
I love you mommy in a tree.

*Figure 8. Mechelle's Pattern Story*

## 22. Phonics—Meaningfully

Nothing has failed more consistently as a reading method than teaching phonics in an isolated manner without having students understand the application or transfer to the real task of reading. For years we have drilled students on isolated sounds and succeeded only in teaching them to parrot the sounds beautifully in a drill but be at a loss as to how to use them in their reading and writing. KidPhonics is a software program that does a fantastic job in using music, which is a most powerful memory aide, to present new letters and sounds in the context of songs and sentences that children will remember and be able to apply. The Waterford Early Reading Program is another one that teaches phonics in a meaningful way and enhances the learning with beautiful graphics and music; this program even tailors the activities to the students' learning styles.

**Procedure:** When using one of these software programs, demonstrate the way it works to your students and have them sing along with you as you all watch the program. Then give them time to explore this program and learn the letters and sounds they need. Word Builder is another helpful program on KidPhonics. Give your students time to explore the program, build their own words and sentences and share them with you and the class by making a presentation.

## 23. Daily Thoughts and Feelings

Emotions and emotional intelligence are a large part of who we are, and students need time to explore their feelings in writing. Writing about their own thoughts and feelings and their daily lives is what most authors from the young to the experienced do best. It is an important step in developing an "inner voice" as a writer.

**Procedure:** Recognize that a student's writing begins at a very basic exploration stage. Encourage the students to write their names and the names of their family members or pets and words familiar to them. As the students read back their stories and listen to the computer read them, they naturally begin to edit and reflect on the stories. They begin to develop stories that tell more about their personal ideas, lives or adventures.

Read *Alexander and the Terrible, Horrible, No Good, Very Bad Day* by Judith Viorst (Viorst 1972). Discuss Alexander's day and what went wrong with it. Suggest students write about their best day or worst day or perhaps both. With daily practice, students begin to write complex personal stories. Remember *it is a daily activity* and the students are in control of writing about their own experiences, interests and topics they wish to explore. This is what makes the process so empowering to them. You must be a keen observer and have them read what they have written to you and nudge them through your suggestions to write more and expand their writing and reading skills. Make sure they read their finished work to at least three other people in the classroom. Keep the examples of their daily work in a portfolio and use them for parent conferencing; let students pick their favorite writings to bring home and read to their parents.

## ⟡ 24. Journal/Daily Writings: What Happened Today in My Life

**Procedure:** Have students begin their pages with the *Month*, *Day* and *Year*, which they can copy from your classroom calendar. Then encourage them to write their personal experiences, observations and reflections about what is going on in their lives at home, at school, with friends—everything that is important to them. See Figure 9 for an example of a personal story.

Consider themes for each month; for example, in January, discuss New Year's resolutions and have the children think about and write their own. In February, let them create their own valentines to send to friends. On their birthday, let them write the plans for their birthday party or a biographical story about their life. Or perhaps they could write about the wishes they will make when they blow out their birthday candles. November is a perfect time for them to write about what they are thankful for, and, of course, December is the time to write those Christmas lists and letters to Santa. Every month of the year offers topics and ideas for letters of appreciation and celebration to be written by each child.

Shannon

My Cat

I love my cat I like to pet
him. he is A fun cat he chases
string sometimes he gos crazy. he
chaess me.  when my hands  get cold
I rub my fingers through his
soft fer.  I love my cat.
he likes to fight with the cat
across the fense they jump at
oneanuther if you try to pet him
he will try to bight you.

*Figure 9. My Cat Story*

## ☞ 25. Informational Writing

**Procedure:** *Jigsaw* is an activity where you have each student gather a bit of information about a topic and then the group puts it together as a written or computer presentation. For example, if the topic is Animals, each child can focus on her favorite animal, read about that animal and then write a description of the animal, where it lives, what it likes to eat, etc. The students can illustrate their reports or actually find a picture of the animal on the Encarta Encyclopedia and print it out to accompany the reports. They can share their individual reports with one another, help each other edit them, and then present the topic to the class as a group.

Always encourage students to read what they have written to at least three persons in the classroom. Reading their work to classmates is a valuable editing step; as the student rereads it, she will notice omissions, corrections and changes to make.

## ☞ 26. Expert Topic Writing

**Procedure:** All students have their own special interests, and all can become experts on a topic that they get to select and develop. Talk to them about their own special hobbies, interests, favorite sports, movies, books, games, foods, animals, etc. Brainstorm these ideas and list them on the board. Have students choose their area of interest and start writing a piece on what their special interest is, why they chose it, and when they first got interested in it.

Next have them write why they think this interest is important, what they now know about it and what they want to learn about it.

This will be an ongoing project until the authors have included everything they feel needs to be said about their topic, and they become a classroom EXPERT on the topic. In the future when people want more information on this topic, they will consult this EXPERT. Nicholas and Matthew were our airplane experts; see the story they wrote in our first-grade classroom (Figure 10).

Nicholas    Top Gun Illustrated
by Mathew written by
Nicholas
I had a rocket that goes 1000 feet
up in the sky    .If you had one of
these  you would go waco ok. I
want to tell you a story about jets.
Wants I had a rocket that youstoo
bellong to the Army.   The Army
took it and I went with it. They
had 10000 000 jets.  They even had
the f14.    All of them had  5000  000
000  000  missells  in  them the  size
of the sillver bullet. The Navy    had
the same things as the Army. The
Navy had 270000 tanks  so  did  the
Army.   There was 1,0000,000 men. The
men had bazookas, rifles and bombs.
I was in the war too. My rocket blew
up a jet. BOOOOOOOOM! The Man that
was in the jet blew up. The Navy
took the guns  and  bombs and evrey
thing they had. The Navy  had  wun
that war but the Army will win the
next time. You will see the next
war. The Army is a good team. The
Navy is a good team to. My rocket
did blow up when my rocket blew up
that jet.   A war  came  agin. Tanks
were out. Jets were flying to. The
war couldn't be stopped. Many got
kiled. I axudentley sneezed and I
had a mach in my hand. The mach cot
on fire and I dropped it. The ground
was on fire.  I  was  trapped! It was
terubel. My Mom and Dad went to my
funeral when I dide. The Army was
sad to but the Navy was happy
cowubungu dood they said tubyubloor
dood they said a lot of funny
words. You no there was a lot of

wars. Another war came and this time
it couldn't be stopped. The Army
was wining that war. The Navy saw a
air craft kereeer with jets and
tanks and other stuff that they kere
kereeer. The kereeer  is  a  fierce
fighter and a-6E INTRUDER went out
to fight. The intruder got bloon up
by the PANAVIA TORNADO.
peace chapter 2
The Navy  said  let  there  be  peace
umung  us  all  there  was peace for a
little wille for that little while
the men went home.
Hint if  the peace brakes  the  earth
will blo up if the earth blose up
they will dy and the story will
end.Or the F-7 night hok will save
the day.  I no that the F-7 Night
hock will save the day. Air kraft
keeerers because they are big!
things. The would fit the siz of 3
big buses  the  buses  are big.
Back To The War.
the war is a dangerous thin to live
whith. The peace was broken now the
world didin't blow up. But the world
was geting beet up.  If the earth
will blow up it will fail.
chapter 3 name of jets.
hot  wings  2
F-5 TIGER II
FB-111
AV-8B HARRIER II
A-6E INTRUDER
AH-64 APACHE
PANAVIA TORNADO
B-1B BOMBER
A-10 THUDERBOLT II
T-38 TALON
A-7 CORSAIR II

*Figure 10. Top Gun Story*

# ✂ 27. Book Talk

**Procedure:** After they read a self-selected favorite book, have each student create a commercial, sales pitch or creative presentation on why they liked the book. Talk to them about persuasive writing and have a contest to see who can sell the most books.

Students each present their book talk in front of the class. After they have heard all presentations, the class votes on the book choices they would purchase or want to read next. Keep a file of all these book talks, so students can go to the computer and access them and have the computer read the book talks back to them when they are searching for their next good read.

# ✂ 28. How-To Books: Every Child an Expert—KWL Technique

The KWL technique is a method of creating a chart with three categories. The first column is What we already Know about a topic, the next column is What we Want to know and the last column is What we have Learned. The objective is to have students learn how to organize information and conduct simple research by using this technique.

**Procedure:** Show your students how you construct a chart to help you organize information and find out what you need to know. Using your computer, construct a chart like the following or one on another topic that you and your students are interested in.

Share nonfiction books with your students, books written by people who are experts in a particular area. Discuss your chart with the students and have them think of other information to add. Explain how, as we study about a subject in depth, we can become an expert on it and then share our knowledge with others through our oral reports and reports written on the computer that others can read and listen to.

Students in your classroom each have many personal interests and can become an expert on the subject of interest to them if you encourage them and guide them to read about the topic and become an expert. Ask students to create their own KWL charts on their topics. Have them share with the class what they are learning about their favorite topic and write on the computer what they know about the subject, what they are learning about it and what they still want to find out.

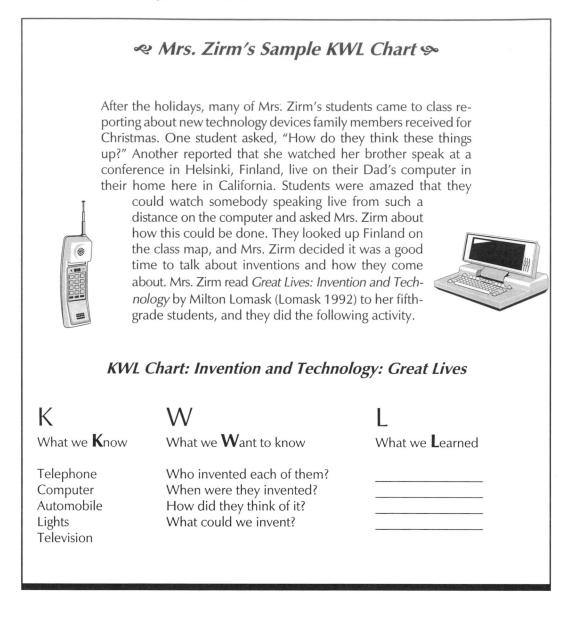

## ✑ *Mrs. Zirm's Sample KWL Chart* ✑

After the holidays, many of Mrs. Zirm's students came to class reporting about new technology devices family members received for Christmas. One student asked, "How do they think these things up?" Another reported that she watched her brother speak at a conference in Helsinki, Finland, live on their Dad's computer in their home here in California. Students were amazed that they could watch somebody speaking live from such a distance on the computer and asked Mrs. Zirm about how this could be done. They looked up Finland on the class map, and Mrs. Zirm decided it was a good time to talk about inventions and how they come about. Mrs. Zirm read *Great Lives: Invention and Technology* by Milton Lomask (Lomask 1992) to her fifth-grade students, and they did the following activity.

### KWL Chart: Invention and Technology: Great Lives

| K | W | L |
|---|---|---|
| What we **K**now | What we **W**ant to know | What we **L**earned |
| Telephone | Who invented each of them? | _____ |
| Computer | When were they invented? | _____ |
| Automobile | How did they think of it? | _____ |
| Lights | What could we invent? | _____ |
| Television | | |

Publish these reports as books. Bind them with simple three-hole punch binding and have the students illustrate or use computer graphics or magazine pictures to create a cover. Have students include a byline, dedication, table of contents and simple index at the back of the book so that they learn the essential parts of a book. These books can be displayed at open house and then kept on a library shelf in the classroom for all to enjoy.

## ❧ 29. *Biographies—All About Me*

**Procedure:** Listen to the conversation at any party—people love to talk about themselves and what is happening in their lives. We all have our own personal story to tell and it is important for us to have someone to tell it to. The classroom is the perfect place for students to share what is happening in their lives.

Read books about a child's life, such as *Tom Sawyer*.

Write a short biography of your life that you show to your students on the computer and projection monitor, and point out some of the important elements you included.

Encourage students to begin a file on the computer with their names and to write in this file things that they can remember about their lives in their early years, what they are doing now and what they hope for the future. Tell them this is a project that they can work on all year, adding to this file when they have new important events happen or when they remember something they want to include. Periodically ask students to share what they have written so far. Use this as an end-of-the-year project that will be printed out, bound, illustrated and taken home for their families to enjoy and the students to keep.

## ❧ 30. *All About Us—Group Project*

**Procedure:** Read a book about a class or school group or write a sample short story about how you as a teacher see this class. Talk about what you see as strengths of this particular group and encourage them to form teams to write about their class. One team could create brief biographies of each student; one team could write about the projects done in class; one team could write about field trips or school events; one team could write about the community; one team could write about their teacher. The final chapter tells what makes your class the very best. Publish the book in class and donate it to the school library.

## ❧ 31. *All About Books—Group Project*

**Procedure:** This activity could work well when you are studying a theme or unit in class as a group. Suppose the subject is the hospital, which one first-grade class at Tustin Ranch Elementary School, in Tustin, California, recently studied. The Ranch pupils opened up a "hospital" to conclude a project advancing reading and writing skills; the nineteen first-graders turned their classroom into a hospital as part of a month-long school project. Students learned what it takes to operate a hospital by interviewing doctors, nurses, paramedics and pharmacists. The business-minded students also applied for a City Hall building permit. The children led city and school officials through a radiation center, an operating room, a nursery and a pharmacy.

**All About A Hospital**

This is the perfect kind of a project to culminate in an "All About . . ." Book Project—"All About A Hospital" by First-Grade Students. Each child contributes information they have learned from interviews, listening, reading and experiencing. They write on the talking computer and illustrate their work on the computer, by hand or with acquired pictures. The class should work as a cooperative group on this project, having editors for each chapter, illustrators to collect illustrations and design the cover of the book, etc.

## ✎ 32. Family Stories

**Procedure:** Read the story *The Relatives Came* by Cynthia Rylant, a Caldecott Award–winning book (Rylant 1986). This story communicates both the exuberance and exhaustion of a family reunion. As in all cultures, one of the family's first jobs is to persuade its members they're special. The stories shared around the family dinner table prove that we are indeed stronger, braver, tougher, wiser, wittier, more talented, sensitive, better looking than all the rest (Stillman 1989). Share some of your family stories with your students and then let them go to the computers and write down some of  their own family stories to share with the class or in a class book.

## ✎ 33. Dreams: What I Want to Be Someday and Why

We all have dreams, hopes, aspirations, ideas of what we would like to be someday. Jessica had dreams of winning the Olympics and she wrote the following story (Figure 11). Share this story with your students and then suggest that they write about their dream or what they would like to be someday.

The Vois Inside You

One day Jenny seid to her mom I want to do jimnastiks
Her mom seid ok why dont you try out for the Olimpiks? Jennys techer was tuf.
It was the day of the Olimpiks. Jenny was scard when it came to her tern.
Then she herd a vois it seid you can do it.
Jenny ran to the beem.
She did a back flip.
the vois cep saing you can do it.
Then it came agen you can do it.
She one the Olimpks

By Jessica
Kindergarten

*Figure 11. The Vois Inside You Story*

**Procedure:** Once again, as a teacher you want your students to know that you are a writer as well, so write a story about one of your dreams or aspirations. Share your story with your students. Now ask them to think about what they want to be someday and go to the computer and write and then illustrate their story.

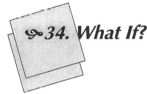

## ✎ 34. What If?

**Procedure:** Encourage your students to write about if they were different people of their choice. Once they decide who they are, they can write a What If story about being in different places. Where in the World Is Carmen San Diego? (Broderbund 1999) is

### What If I Was a Space Explorer

### *by Will Casey*

If I was a space explorer I could find new worlds. I would ride in my spaceship and wave to the earth, if I was a space explorer I would learn many new things.

a very good software program to use along with this activity. After they explore places, they could write their What If story on KidWorks Deluxe talking word processor.

## ॐ35. *Friendship*

**Procedure:** For the Primary Grades, read the classic books by Arnold Lobel on friendship. *Frog and Toad Are Friends* (Lobel 1970) is the first of the series. These books exemplify friendship, acceptance, and reliability in a timeless setting. Discuss the story and then have students brainstorm with you what qualities they like to have in a friend. Write this list on the board. Then have the students go to the computer and write a story about a best friend they have or one they would like to have.

For Middle Grades, read *Sadako and the Thousand Paper Cranes* by Eleanor Coerr (Coerr 1999). It is a true story about a girl who died of leukemia as a result of radiation from the atom bomb. Her friends' support during her illness is an outstanding example of friendship. Have your students discuss the components of true friendship and then write about a friend who really stood by them when they needed it.

Socially some students have a great deal of difficulty making new friends; others feel left out because they are different. Read the story *Crow Boy* by Taro Yashima (Yashima 1955). This story is about a lonely child who develops competence in some field and so wins the admiration and acceptance of the group. Discuss the story as a group. Ask students to write about a time they felt left out and why and how someone helped them to feel accepted. Break the class into cooperative groups and have each group brainstorm and come up with a list of how to be a good friend. Have one person in each group put the list on the computer and another person from the group give a presentation to the class about how they decided on their list. The last person prints out the list and brings it to the publishing center to be put into a class book.

> ➤ *The following activities (36–41) discuss the kinds of letter-writing opportunities available from personal correspondence to electronic penpals and to relatives, to daily messages to classmates or teacher.*

## ❧36. *Correspondence—Meaningful Communication— Locally, Nationally, Globally*

Hillary Rodham Clinton has written a book called *Dear Socks, Dear Buddy* (Clinton 1998), which includes letters from children to the First Family's pets. Mrs. Clinton emphasizes to parents the importance of writing to children's development. As teachers you know the key to letter writing is that the letters are meaningful to the child, and not just a letter that is copied out of a textbook as an assignment.

**Procedure:** Encourage your students to write letters to their significant others: parents, grandparents, siblings, etc. Encourage them to let these people who are important in their lives know this. Demonstrate a group letter that you write to your students telling them how important they are to you.

## ❧37. *Electronic Penpals or Snail Mail Buddies*

When I was nine years old, Miss Carver, my wonderful fourth-grade teacher, encouraged us all to write to a penpal in some far-off part of the world. She obtained names and addresses of students our age from an organization called the International Penpal Club. I chose to write to a nine-year-old girl from Tasmania, Australia, named Leita Weller. My parents helped me locate Tasmania, a small island south of Australia, on the globe. It was on the other side of the world; when we were having winter, she was experiencing summer. Would this girl's life be anything like mine? I waited anxiously for a reply. Several weeks passed and at last I received that first letter. I had a new friend, and her experiences were a window into the life of someone my age on the other side of the world. I was hooked.

I have written to Leita now for fifty years. We both have albums full of pictures we have exchanged through the years, but the best part of the story happened four years ago when my husband and I traveled to Tasmania and met Leita and her husband. We stayed at their house for four days, and they showed us the sights of their island. We fed kangaroos from our hand, we saw the emu farm across the road from them, we met many wonderful Australian people, but most of all we got to spend time with our friends across the world—and all because of Miss Carver and her plan to encourage her students to do meaningful writing and discover new friends and connections in the world. This was a priceless gift for me; and you can give this gift to every one of your students.

**Procedure:** Start by visiting the following Internet sites:

http://www.stolaf.edu

This site lists 3,041 subscribers from 57 countries participating in a classroom penpal list service.

http://www.iwaynet.net

This site has a school listing section that is an alphabetical listing (by country) of schools wanting to exchange penpal letters with other schools. It also allows you to join the penpal exchange.

You, the teacher, need to preview these sites and resources and make sure you choose ones that will meet the needs of your students. Snail mail, or having the students write their letters on the computer but mail them to the students' homes, is a good way to start. Let them use their home addresses so even students without a computer at home can receive mail from a friend.

The other option, of course, is e-mail (electronic mail) if you have a computer with a dedicated line in your classroom. Students can visit that center daily to send or receive e-mail messages from their penpals around the world.

The benefits of this activity are many. The first and most obvious is the benefit of having a real person your age to write to and share stories of your life with. This kind of confidant can really be important for students who feel they don't have friends in class or can't share something with people they see daily. The other important benefit is making friends with students globally and realizing we all have many important things in common in our lives and how important it is for us to respect and value people from all cultures.

## ❧38. Letters for Information or Action— "Things Children Can Write For"

**Procedure:** The talking word processor in the classroom is the perfect tool to empower students to include in their daily writing letters to request information for something they want to learn about, and also to register their opinions about things happening in the world that they wish to be heard about. Use Judith Viorst's book *If I Were in Charge of the World* (Viorst 1981). Encourage your students to write letters to the editor or to the President on how they think we could have a better world.

*Teacher Model:* Bring in some letters to the editor written to magazines. Share these letters with your students and explain how in a free society we can write our opinions and have them published so others can read them. Have your students write a letter to the President about the environment, or letters to the local newspaper about issues they feel are important to young people their age.

Students should print them out and mail them as a group or individually to await responses. Construct a bulletin board in your classroom titled, "We Care, We Speak Out!" and display the letters. Take a field trip to the town newspaper; talk to the editor of the newspaper about how important people's opinions are to the community.

## ❧ 39. Letters to Persuade or Complain

**Procedure:** Read *Earrings* by Judith Viorst (Viorst 1993) to your class. Ask your students how the girl felt about having earrings and her reasons for wanting them. Talk about the arguments she used to persuade her parents. Suggest to your students that they think of something they want very much, then write a letter describing what it is they want and why it is so important to them. Guide them through developing a persuasive argument. Let students discuss and share examples and then deliver their letter to those involved.

## ❧ 40. Letters to Receive Free or Inexpensive Materials

**Procedure:** It's always fun to receive things in the mail. Have your students use the computer to write for some of the free or inexpensive materials found in the following books. They should share the materials they receive with the class. Using the Internet and the search engine AltaVista, look up Free & Inexpensive Materials for Teachers to discover many resources. One Web site to visit is

www.lib.virginia.edu/education/free.htm

The books listed below all list free and inexpensive materials teachers and parents can obtain by contacting the publisher of the material.

*Editors:* Harrington, Barry, and Beth Christensen
*Title:* Unbelievably Good Deals That You Absolutely Can't Get Unless You're a Teacher
*Publisher:* Chicago, IL: Contemporary Books, 1997

*Title:* Free Stuff for Kids
*Publisher:* Deephaven, MN: Meadowbrook Press, 1997

*Author:* Osborne, Susan
*Title:* Free (and Almost Free) Things for Teachers
*Publisher:* New York: Putnam, 1993

## ✎41. Letters to a Story Book Character or an Author

**Procedure:** Read the *Jolly Postman* by Janet and Allan Ahlberg (Ahlberg 1986) to your students; talk about the letters in that book. Talk about their favorite characters in a book or their favorite books. An interesting activity can be done online using cross-age tutors. Have a middle-school class agree to respond to primary-grade students' letters to a favorite story book character. This can be done online from room to room or school to school or through the mail.

Read *Dear Mr. Henshaw* (Cleary 1984) when doing this activity with older students. Encourage students to write to their favorite book author. You can address the letters to the author in care of the publishing company or look the company up on the Web.

---

Smith Elementary School
March 11, 2000
Theodore Taylor
Laguna Beach, CA

Dear Mr. Taylor,

The Cay was one of your books that I really loved, thank you for coming to our class and speaking about it. Hope you write lots more books about Timothy, I liked him a lot wish I had his adventures.

Sincerely,
Kevin Casey
Grade 5

---

## ✎42. The Publishing Classroom

*News in the twenty-first century—Your classroom is a microcosm of the community. Events happen that are news.*

**Procedure:** Create a model newsroom in your classroom. The first step is to see if you can arrange a trip to the local newspaper office so that students can see how a paper operates in the real world. Arrange to have papers delivered to your classroom weekly. Help your students learn to read the newspaper and then write about what they have found interesting that day or about their favorite section. Now you are ready to begin creating your own classroom newsroom.

*Primary Grades.* Students can write simple stories about the class experiences, poems, jokes and create a newsletter for the class.

*Middle School.* Students can create a weekly class newspaper or write the script for a weekly TV class news show, done on video or multimedia using HyperStudio software, that they will film and present to the class each Friday.

# ✑43. *Classroom Newsletter*

**Procedure:** You need an editor, reporters, writers and photo coordinators to put together an effective classroom newsletter. Have students apply for these positions, and change the staff every few months to give many students the opportunity to participate in this activity.

*Editor.* The chief task of the editor is to assign the stories to the reporters and read and edit the stories turned in by the writer. You as the teacher should be the editor-in-chief and pass the final approval of what the student editor submits to you. The audience for your newsletter is the class but also parents and other classes in the school.

*Reporters.* The chief task of the reporters is to gather the news. This is a wonderful opportunity to have students learn interviewing skills—finding out the who, what, where, when and why (5 Ws) information they need to know to write effective news stories. They could collaborate with another student reporter or a cross-age peer tutor from a higher grade when putting the information they have gathered together as a story. They can present interviews of special people to the class. The reporters should select someone in the school or community for a weekly interview to appear in the newsletter.

*Writers.* Headlines, titles and information pieces that don't require interviews can be written by these students.

*Photo Coordinators.* The main job of photographers is to take pictures, scan them and format them. This is a job for your artistic, visual learners to apply their skills.

The *Newsletter* can be produced weekly, monthly—whatever your class decides—but once a week show the completed copy on the projection monitor for the whole class to view. Let the talking computer read articles, let students read along or view their own copy as they watch the large group presentation. This will give everyone the news, but it's also good reading practice for those in your class who need lots of opportunities to see good writing, hear good writing and read along with others. This is especially great for your second-language learners, for it makes a very comprehensible activity.

*Morning News or Current Events.* Place a student in charge of typing on the computer each morning the morning news, latest current events or notice of special events happening in school or the community. Project this news for the students, print them each a copy and let the talking computer read it aloud as students follow along on their copies. This is the perfect daily, multisensory type of meaningful activity that is essential to developing writers and readers.

## ✖44. Our Class Web Page

**Procedure:** Show your students the Nightingale Web Page included here (Figure 12); you can also find it at

http://orcutts1.sbceo.k12.ca.us/public/nightingale/index.htm

Search to find other Web pages from classes of their age level. Put together a group in your class interested in creating their own Web page. Select a Webmaster and a team of writers to gather the information for the Web page. Have them type out the information they want on it. You are the final editor to give the last stamp of approval before the material is posted. Post this information on your school Web site.

## ✖45. The Art of Writing Fiction

**Procedure:** Invite a local author to your classroom. Theodore Taylor, who wrote *The Cay*, frequently visits classrooms and talks to the children about how he writes his books and answers their questions about where he gets his ideas to write. Let the students ask him about how he does his writing. Contact your local library to find out about available authors in your community.

Read several fiction books to your students. Have them choose one of their favorite stories and then try to write a story of their own with a similar structure to the story that they like so much.

Encourage students to try writing their own fiction story. Talk about the fact that they can create the setting, characters and story line. Now, your students are ready to go to the computer and begin creating this first novel. It will take time but they can continue it daily, making sure to revise as they go along. Watch out, best-selling authors! The students from your class on are their way!

As a teacher, you might try writing a fiction story yourself and sharing it with them.

Joe Nightingale School

# Welcome to Joe Nightingale School's Student Created Home Page!

## Reaching Our Dreams Through Learning

Welcome to Joe Nightingale School's home page! Our school is located in Orcutt CA, in the Santa Maria Valley. We have over seven hundred students, the most in the district! Joe Nightingale School is a California Distingushed School and a National Blue Ribbon School! We are creating this home page to let people know about the interesting aspects of our community and school. You can learn about the:

| Chumash Indians | California Missions | Central Coast Sealife |
|---|---|---|
| Interesting School Activities | School and Local Information | Classroom Happenings |
| Internet Club | Student Art Gallery | Odyssey of the Mind |

## Take a Tour Around Santa Maria!

☺

## Meet our community partner

The information for our home page was researched, written and designed by over fifty Joe Nightingale students. Not only did they use the Internet to gather information via email and the World Wide Web, but they also learned how to write a Hyper Text Markup Language document, use a scanner, along with a digital camera, to enhance their web sites. We hope you enjoy all of their hard work!

Let us know what you think of our home page. Our address is:

*Joe Nightingale School 255 Winter Road Santa Maria, CA 93455*
*eagles@nightingale.sbceo.k12.ca.us*

*Figure 12. Joe Nightingale School Web Page. Reprinted by permission.*

## ✎ 46. Animal Stories

**Procedure:** Read *Charlotte's Web* by E. B. White (White 1999) to your class. It's a wonderful story told through the eyes of a spider, pig and other animals. Visit this Web site to see the wonderful work done by a second-grade class after their teacher read them this story:

http://www2.lhric.org/pocantico/charlotte/index.htm

Have students choose an animal they know about, perhaps their pet, and write what they think the animal might think about, and imagine adventures that their animal might have. Have them write about and draw this animal and then share their stories with one another. See Figure 13.

I have a    gerbil.
Some times he bits my thumb.   Alvin
is growing up.   3 days after cristmas
he will be 2.   I cant wait.    That is
the first pet I ever had.
I might get    another pet. Some times
when I pick him up he droops at both
ends and some times he falls out of
your hand.
                    Faith

*Figure 13. Faith's Gerbil Story*

## ✎ 47. Fractured Fairy Tales

**Procedure:** Jon Scieszka's books, *The Stinky Cheese Man* and *The True Story of the Three Little Pigs* (Scieszka 1992, 1989), are perfect ones to start this activity. Discuss the point of view of the different characters in the stories. Talk about whose point of

view is reflected by the storyteller. For example, in "Little Red Riding Hood," we hear the story through her eyes, but what about the wolf's story—what might his point of view be? Have the students choose one of their favorite fairy tale books and write a story from a different character's point of view, such as "The Three Billy Goats Gruff" told by the troll. A fifth-grade class wrote a mock trial with the Billy Goat family suing the troll for not allowing them to cross the bridge; there were lawyers for both sides. The students wrote out the script for each side on the computer and added graphics that they used in their presentations.

## 48. Sports Stories

**Procedure:** This is a very important section, for it is often sports or books about sports stars that "hook a student on books." Remember that we learn when we are interested or need to know. Your classroom needs to be full of books such as *Baseball Saved Us* by Ken Mochizuki (Mochizuki 1993) and other sport stories; you'll find lists of them in *Children's Books and Their Creators* by Anita Silvey (Silvey 1995). Encourage the students' interest by reading to your class a book such as *Casey at the Bat* by Ernest Thayer (Thayer 1988).

Suggest to students that they think of their favorite sport and write a story on the computer about how they played that sport and what happened in the game. The sky's the limit to their imagination. Tell them they can end up on an Olympic team in their story—whatever dream they can think of, they can write about.

## 49. Tall Tales

**Procedure:** The characteristic of the tall tale that makes it different from other humorous stories is its blatant exaggeration. Children love humor and exaggeration. *Paul Bunyon* by Steven Kellogg (Kellogg 1984) has got to be one of the best books in this area. Paul's blue ox, Babe, measures "forty-two ax handles between the eyes."

Another book to read to your students is *Cloudy with a Chance of Meatballs* by Judi Barrett (Barrett 1982), a wonderful weather story of the day it rained spaghetti.

Read a book from this genre to your students and then challenge them to make a really fantastic, exaggerated story and type it on the computer. They can share their tall tale with the class by having the computer read the story back to the entire group.

## ❧50. *Mystery Stories*

**Procedure:** One of the most popular genres of reading for adults is the mystery story. Children share that interest. The virtues of good mystery tales for children are numerous. Children like the atmosphere of excitement and suspense, and these books become the most tempting of all baits for nonreaders. Witness the phenomenal success of *Harry Potter and the Sorcerer's Stone* by J. K. Rowling (Rowling 1998). This series of books has been on the *New York Times* best-seller lists for many weeks. From age nine up, children are eagerly waiting the next in this exciting mystery, magical series. Television-generation children demand highly spiced book fare if they are going to read at all. The overwhelming popularity of the R. L. Stine *Goosebumps* books (Stine 1997) attests to that.

Always remember our goal is to hook our students on books and be the catalyst for their becoming lifelong readers. For your daily reading to your class, choose an exciting chapter book in an adventure or mystery series. *The Boxcar Children* by Gertrude Chandler Warner (Warner 1942) was the series of books that hooked my granddaughter Katie in first grade and turned her into an avid reader, plaintively asking her mom, "Can we drive to the bookstore? I am ready for book #5 now!"

## ❧51. *Adventure Stories*

**Procedure:** Another very popular type of story for adults and children alike is the true-life adventure, such as Jon Krakauer's *Into Thin Air* (Krakauer 1997), about his perilous journey climbing Mount Everest. *Curious George* by H. A. Rey (Rey 1973) is about an adventurous tailless monkey, who has a lively curiosity about the world around him. Read several of these books to your students, and encourage them to think about some of the adventures they have had in their lives. We all have stories to tell about real-world events that have happened in our lives.

Make your writing classroom a risk-free place where children feel safe to write and tell their true stories. Your students are capable of writing much more, and with greater depth and understanding, than you ever imagined. Look at Elizabeth's story—she is only a first-grader and yet she wrote this adventure story about a diver (see Figure 14). If she can do it, so can your students.

---

## DANGER BELOW

Once a diver went underneath the ocean to find gold. He jumped off. Then he saw a shark. It was a great white.But it said, "Don't  be afraid. I won't hurt you.   I am a dolphin with a great white costume on.I bought it from Mr. Octupus. So I won't  hurt you. What are you looking for, anyway?"
The diver said, "I am a diver looking for gold." The dolphin said, "I            know where the gold is." So the dolphin took the diver by his hand and led him to the gold.
When they got there the diver said,"How will I repay you?" The dolphin replied,"By love."
So every day   the diver   went to the dolphins house.

Elizabeth

---

*Figure 14. Danger Below Story*

## ✂ 52. *Fantasy Story*

**Procedure:** Read your class a story such as *The Runaway Bunny* by Margaret Wise Brown (Brown 1974) and other animal adventures. Then encourage them to create their own story on the computer.

Mary is a five-year-old whose favorite animal was a bunny. Read the exciting story she wrote about a bunny who ran away (see Figure 15).

Mary:

The Bunny Who Ran Away

One day in bunny land hopse
was soso mad at the uther
bunnys she ran away.  She went
sterat to  Bun Buns  house. She said
lets run away.Bun Bun  said o.k.
but I do not know why. Hopse
said be cos the other  bunnes
always say names about us. hopse
said hay  les go. Its omost moring
so stop tocing and  git on are
way be for  they  star loocing for
us. rit when he said  that  his mom
fowndowt she calld the  ples but
thay wer at  a fier  but thay herd it
on c.b.  and  stad  on the look
for them.  they  fownd  them and took
them hom. Wol they wer  in the
car they fell a slep  their  mom
was happy.

*Figure 15. The Bunny Who Ran Away Story*

## ꙮ53. Re-Telling Favorite Stories (Assessing Comprehension)

**Procedure:** Our lives are made up of the stories we live. Every child has a rich resource of stories in her head; it is your job to share your own personal stories and then, through appropriate questioning and interest, bring out the child's own life stories and encourage the child to use these as the source of her daily writing.

This activity is especially important, for through re-telling of stories, we can assess the comprehension ability of our students. One way to do it is to read a favorite story to your class, ask them to go to the computer and write all they can remember about the story, re-tell it and illustrate it. Not only is this a fun activity, but it can serve as a re-telling assessment of comprehension for you to keep in their portfolio.

## ✎54. Movies and Videos

**Procedure:** Your students certainly all have a TV and many watch videos of all the Disney films at home and, of course, many go to the movies with their families. These experiences provide you with a rich resource for children's writing. Suggest students write about their favorite movie, video or TV shows they have seen.

Remember to first share an example of your writing about a favorite movie or television program that you show to the whole class on the projection monitor. Have the talking computer read the story to the group.

Another idea is to have your students read a book about King Arthur and then watch the movie *Excalibur*; discuss with the students the similarities and differences in the book and the movie.

## ✎55. Creating Movies and Videos

**Procedure:** This is the next step and especially appropriate for the gifted learners in your class who want to take creativity a step beyond. I have seen second graders successfully using a video camera to create their own video film. This takes lots of planning and writing but your creative students will be engrossed in this activity. Share with them model play or movie scripts, then encourage them to write a script on the computer and film their production from the script.

> *The Art of Writing Non-Fiction (Activities 56–57)*

# ❧56. Science Reports and Books

Science, whether it's animals, the ocean, rocks and minerals, or the stars and planets, have fascinated humans for all time and your students will have their own particular interests. Using the Internet for research and the talking computer to write their reports gives students the support they need to find information and then write about what they have learned.

**Procedure:** A KWL strategy works well here. Have the students pick the topic of greatest interest to them, for example, Rocks and Minerals (my big interest in sixth grade), then have them start by writing all they: **Know** about the topic, what they **Want** to learn and then as they do their research, **what they have Learned**. This can turn into a report or a book compiled from the science research of all your students.

# ❧57. Social Studies Reports and Books

**Procedure:** Once again the I-search method rather than an assigned report is most powerful here. *I search* is seeking out information you are interested in and need to know; often an assigned report is one you HAVE to do and hope to forget about as quickly as possible once the assignment is turned in. As human beings and learners, we need choice and control in our learning. This does not mean that guidance from the teacher is not needed or that certain curriculum topics will not be studied, but it does mean that students will have the option to choose to focus on the area they are interested in pertaining to the topic.

For example, let's take the Civil War. Some students may choose to focus, research and write about the battles; others may want to find out about the people of that time, how did they dress, what did they eat, etc. There are as many aspects to this topic as there are students in your class and based on their interest, experience or background, you can help them find the idea pertaining to this social studies topic that will inspire them to learn more about it. Then they write a report for the rest of the class to learn from, and having the computer read their report back to the group helps everyone get the information through their best modality of learning.

## ❧ 58. Our Global Neighbors

**Procedure:** Prepare a four-card Hyper-Studio stack as an example for your students, introducing a country that you are interested in. Have the students choose a country on the map or globe that they would like to travel to or find out about. It could be the place where their ancestors came from, it could be a place where they have a penpal or friend or just a place they are interested in knowing about.

The students need to search the Internet to find information about their country; if it is possible to interview someone from that country, they should do that as well. They will write their final report on HyperStudio, making at least an eight-card stack that through the use of text and graphics introduces the rest of the class to that country and the people who live there.

## ❧ 59. Family Tree

**Procedure:** Inspiration software will work nicely on this activity, for it allows you to create a web or concept map. Bring in your own Family Tree or information about your family that you share with your students, perhaps a picture of your grandmother or grandfather. Ask your students to interview their parents and get as much information as they can about their family roots. Once they bring the information in, demonstrate to them how to build a family tree web on Inspiration and let them each create their own. The next step might be to ask them to interview someone on their family tree and write a short biography about that person's life.

## ❧ 60. Directions for Projects, Recipes, How-to-Make Something

**Procedure:** Our lives are full of directions and lists that we need to know or remember in order to do many things: cook food, find our friend's house, build a model airplane, start an American Girl® Club. The list goes on and on.

As the teacher, be aware of these kinds of interests and needs of your students. One idea is to have them do a class recipe book for their mother on Mother's Day. Another is to write a book on how to make things to share with one another, or a book of places to visit in their community. Again give each student guidance and the ability to choose their contribution, write it, and compile the information into a talking as well as a printed class book. Finally, they can share their completed work with each other.

## ❧61. My Favorites

**Procedure:** Play the song, "My Favorite Things," from *The Sound of Music* in your class. Then share with them a list of your favorite things. Have the students go to the computer and create a list of their own favorite things and then share their lists with a small group. Have them save these lists in their portfolio, and then use the topics on the list for future writing projects. Since they will be doing daily writing, they can refer to these lists and write about: my favorite color, food, sport, friend, car, hobby, book, movie, TV show, magazine, toy, video game, board game, clothing, song, rock star, movie star, TV star, animal, vegetable, mineral, planet and on and on. There are many topics that are meaningful to each of us and having a list of them in students' writing portfolio means there will never be a day when they say, "I can't think of anything to write about!"

## ❧62. What Bugs Me

**Procedure:** We all have things that bother us and often feel we are the only ones who feel that way. Discuss with your students some things that bother you, such as people who crunch popcorn in back of you at the movies, people who never turn in their work, people who cut in front of you in line, etc. Let them think of things that bother them as well. Have them each choose their greatest pet peeve and write why it bothers them so much and what they think they might be able to do about it. Have them share these with the group and bind them into a "Pet Peeve" book for the class library.

## 63. Inventions

**Procedure:** At the primary level, Dr. Seuss books can be wonderful inspiration for fun inventions. After reading *The Lorax* (Seuss 1998) to your class, let students create their own fantastic inventions by drawing them, writing about them and then sharing them with one another or the class. At the middle- and upper-grade level, this is the perfect opportunity for students to read about inventors and try and create an idea or invention of their own.

## 64. Writing Menus

**Procedure:** Bring in sample menus from McDonald's and other restaurants that are favorites of your students. Talk about their favorite foods. Have them pick a partner and develop a menu for their own restaurant, have them design a theme for the restaurant and use KidWorks to design graphic signs and ads for the restaurant. Have them create and print out a menu and then present their ideas to the rest of the class.

## 65. Writing Recipes

**Procedure:** Read *The Popcorn Book* by Tomie dePaola (dePaola 1978) to your students and then have a popcorn party in class. Type the recipe for popcorn from the book on your computer and let the students all read it together. Talk about how important it is to get all the ingredients right in a recipe and what would happen if you did not. Then have the students bring in a favorite recipe from home and type it on the computer and write the directions for making it. These recipes can then be bound into "Our Class Recipe Book."

## ✎66. Writing Lists

**Procedure:** All our lives are surrounded by lists: shopping lists, to-do lists, lists of ingredients for cooking, list of directions for finding a place we want to go. You should model one of your own shopping lists for your students, or perhaps your list might be the scheduled activities for the day. Put your list up on the projection monitor for all your students to see. Discuss the many types of lists we use daily. Have each student decide upon the kind of list they need to create, write it on the computer, print it out, take it home and check off as they accomplish things on the list. Here's a list of favorite foods written by a kindergarten student (see Figure 16).

*Figure 16. A Student's Favorite Foods*

## ☙67. *Writing a Travel Brochure*

**Procedure:** Bring in some travel brochures from a travel agency. Discuss the design, layout and text of these brochures. Using HyperStudio or the Ultimate Writing and Creativity Center, challenge your students to pick a place they have traveled to and loved or would like to travel to and create a brochure. They can work in teams or alone on this project. Finished projects can be displayed on a travel bulletin board.

## ☙68. *Writing Poetry*

**Procedure:** Start with the Shel Silverstein book, *Where the Sidewalk Ends* (Silverstein 1974) and share your favorite poems in that book with your students. "Sarah Cynthia Stout Would Not Take the Garbage Out" is one of my favorites. After reading it to your students, let them create their own poem about what would happen at their house if they failed to take the garbage out.

Another great poem in this book is "If I Had a Brontosaurus"; read it to your students and project it for them all to see, then print out copies for them to do a choral reading.

Suggest they create their own "If I Had a [animal of their choice]" poem and share it with the class. You might also read T. S. Eliot's *Old Possum's Book of Practical Cats* (Eliot 1984) and share with your students a poem from that book like "The Naming of Cats." After reading the poem together, suggest they create their own poem based on what they would name their cat and allow them time to illustrate their poem. There is no end to the types of poems you can model.

Try a *cinquain*, which is a poem that is perfect for round-robin poetry writing. It is a five-line poem in which the first line has one word; the second line, two words; the third line, three words; the fourth line, four words; and the fifth line, one.

Today
New Year's
A celebration day
My resolutions won't be
Forgotten

Demonstrate your poem and then encourage the students to write their own.

Other types of poems are:

*Haiku.* Three-line Japanese poem. The first line has five syllables; the second, seven syllables; and the third, five syllables.

*Name Poems.* Students write the letters of their name vertically and then pick out a word that fits each letter. Explore and model many forms of poetry; the book *Families Writing* by Peter R. Stillman (Stillman 1989) has many excellent activity ideas in this area.

## ∾ 69. *Playwriting*

**Procedure:** Students love to make believe and create their own plays. Start with a readers theatre script you share with your class. A good resource to find scripts is on the Web at

http://www.readers-theatre.com/

---

### ∾ *Advantages of Teaching with Readers Theatre* ∾

1.  Motivates learning through entertainment

2.  Requires no special equipment

3.  Easy to use

4.  Successful for all ability levels

5.  Rapid results

6.  Creates cooperative interaction

7.  Adds liveliness to the classroom

8.  Supports other teaching methodologies

9.  Joins creativity to learning

10.  Improves self-image through standard of excellence

11.  Teaches oral and written communication along with subject matter

12.  Repetition reinforces comprehension and retention

Talk about how writing a play is different from writing a story. You need to describe the scene, tell which character is talking and describe their entrances and exits. Then encourage your students to work in teams, create their own plays and present them to the class. The Ultimate Writing and Creativity Center software program from the Learning Company (Learning Company 1998) has a program to write plays and then hear them read back.

## ✎ 70. Writing Movie Reviews

**Procedure:** Poll your students on what movies they like to see and what they have seen lately. Read a review of a current movie to them from the newspaper. Tell them a review of a movie you just saw. Talk about what you all think makes a good movie. Construct a classroom chart "Movies We Have Seen" and ask each child to select one and write a review of this movie. Reviews can be printed out and shared with the class. Let them vote thumbs up or thumbs down on each movie reviewed.

## ✎ 71. Movie Script Writing

**Procedure:** This is definitely a middle-grade activity. Using multimedia software such as HyperStudio, a team of students can actually develop a script and include videos and graphics in their presentation. Your gifted students will especially like the challenge of an activity like this.

Just like every activity in this book, it is important that you model the project first. Try to get an actual scriptwriter to come to your class and tell how he does his job.

The next best thing is for you to prepare a sample project on HyperStudio that you present to the class as an example of the kind of script they can write. Once the students have seen these models and understand the project, let them form teams and develop their scripts and create their movie. The final projects will be presented to the class and maybe even to the parents on a special parent night.

# 72. TV Show Writing

**Procedure:** Do a classroom poll and find out what TV shows the students in your class are watching. This is very important information for you to have in order to understand the background experience and jargon they are learning in the TV environment; find out how many hours a day they watch TV. Discuss fantasy vs. reality with the entire class. Have students give examples of what they see on TV and then talk about whether those things are fantasy or reality.

Have students watch one of their favorite programs and write notes about the story, what happened first, next, etc. Then tell them that their assignment is to pretend they are a TV writer and write the next episode of that show: What do they think will happen next to their favorite characters? Is the story fantasy or reality?

Have students share their final products with the entire class. This is an excellent activity to pair students or to have a group of three to five collaborate on a group project that they will present to the class.

This is an extremely important lesson for this video generation. Students emulate things they see on TV; a four-year-old jumped out of a window after seeing a Superman episode. Students often get the wrong impression of reality, so this is a vital discussion for you to hold in class. By creating a show, students learn about writing fantasy vs. fact.

> ➤ *Throughout history people have attempted to influence, or persuade, others.*

# 73. Writing Advertisements (Propaganda Lesson)

**Procedure:** Just as distinguishing reality from fantasy is very important at all grade levels, recognizing propaganda in the media is important knowledge that your students need to have. Every day they are bombarded with commercials that try to sell products to them; many of the students have not learned to judge the message in the commercials.

Start this lesson with a definition of propaganda and to advertise.

*Propaganda* is one person's or a group's attempt to persuade another person or group to accept a different point of view or action. Its purpose is to further one's own cause or to damage an opposing one.

*Advertise* means to tell about or praise (a product, service, etc.) publicly, through newspapers, handbills, radio, TV and online Web sites so as to make people want to buy it.

Introduce the techniques used by advertisers to persuade consumers and sell their products. See the chart below.

★ **Bandwagon**
"More mothers prefer Zippy cereal than any other brand."

> This method attempts to convince you that the vast majority of people prefer a particular product; it fails to alert you to other options.

★ **Repetition, Jingle, Song**
"Munch, munch, munch a bunch of Crispy Corn Chips."

> Repetition involves a catchy poem, song or jingle you won't forget.

★ **Testimonial/Famous Endorsement**
Joe Samath, football pro says, "I only wear Zikes shoes."

> Commercials by famous people you admire make you believe you will be like that famous person if you take their advice as to what they think you should wear, eat, etc.

★ **Ego/Image or Self-Esteem Building**
"Are you bright enough, strong enough, etc., to buy Punchy cereal?"

> This approach appeals to your desire to be bright, strong, accepted as one of the crowd.

★ **Authority—Professional People Pitch**
"Most doctors agree that Zest bread builds stronger bones and bodies than any other brand."

> The point is to make you feel that a professional person suggests this is best for you.

★ **Snob Appeal**
"Only the coolest kids living in Richville wear Gloria Starbuck jeans."

> This appeals to your desire to be considered a member of the upper class.

★ **Plain Folks**
"The President of Zippy Tea was once a farm girl, but now she enjoys tea with the neighborhood moms."

> This kind of commercial tells you that the president is just one of the family, like you. Therefore, she would never cheat or sponsor an unreliable product.

These are just some of the many techniques used in commercials. Since your students are bombarded with thousands of hours of TV a year and twenty minutes out of every hour is commercials designed to convince, persuade or sell, it is important that you help them recognize propaganda and sort through the validity of the information they receive daily. (This is a twenty-first-century skill vital to every child.)

*Teacher hint:* Spend a short time taping a few commercials from your TV that demonstrate some of the above approaches. After viewing the commercial, ask the students if they would buy the product and why. Then talk about the following questions they should ask when viewing any commercial.

- Who is trying to sell this product or service?

- Why?

- What method of persuasion are they trying to use?

Give each student a copy of the Propaganda Chart on page 69 that explains the bandwagon, repetition, testimonial, ego/image, authority, snob appeal and plain folk methods. They will use this chart in their activities.

### Computer Activity #1
Using KidWorks Deluxe, have the students each write their own commercials and listen to them read back to them to edit and make sure they are effective. Let them create graphics also to illustrate their commercial and then present it to the class or print it out for a class center or bulletin board on Propaganda.

### Computer Activity #2
Have students take these commercials one step further and videotape them, using the KidWorks Deluxe text as the script. They can present their finished products to the class.

### Computer Activity #3
Using HyperStudio let students create their commercial using video, graphics, sound, music and text available with this product. Have them show their completed commercials to the class.

## ✑ 74. *Campaigning for a Class Office*

**Procedure:** In a democratic classroom, having class officers helps students gain ownership of the environment and also take responsibility for it. Have students listen to campaign speeches on TV or read reports about them in the newspaper. Talk about the similarity between these speeches and an advertisement. Someone is trying to sell you their ideas.

Have a student decide on a class office he would like to run for and write a short campaign speech that explains his qualifications and why he is the best possible person for the job. Have him make campaign posters as well, and then have an election for the office. Elect officers monthly so all students get to have the experience.

Keep a bound book of "Our Class Officers" that contains the printed-out campaign speeches of each candidate. During election time, assign a group of students to report on the candidates running for office so that students can debate the qualifications of the candidates and run a mock election in the classroom.

Have your students visit the following Web site to see how real campaigns are advertised on the Web: http://www.caseydorin.com. Students may wish to create their own Web campaign.

## ❧ 75. Ethics and Social Responsibility (Vital Personal Concerns for Your Students)

**Procedure:** Teachers need to understand the cognitive and affective domains and personalize computer education, and then focus on the interpersonal and broader social contexts of the technology.

> What you would really like to do is instill in your students ethics and a sense of responsibility. We must attend more closely to the development of the whole child for we are at a time when the computer revolution empowers children to enter and affect the adult world in significant ways. We must work alongside them to help them direct this power in positive ways for themselves as well as our society.
>
> —(Marcus 1999)

➢ *Activities 76–78 are some ways to do that.*

## ❧ 76. Self-Identity

**Procedure:** Using KidWorks Deluxe, have K-3 students make a book starting with a drawing of:

This is my family and I.
  I am important to my family because. . . .
This is my class and I.
  I am important to my class because. . . .

This is my community and I.
   I am important to my community because. . . .
This is the United States of America and I.
   I am an important American because. . . .
This is the world and I.
   I am important to the world because. . . .

Print out and gather everyone's work together to make a "We Are Important Human Beings" Class Book. Here's the most important part: let them each present their work and discuss the responsibilities we each have to all these communities in our lives.

Share this book with parents at open house. Explain to them how they must join you in this responsibility to help guide the next generation in the development of human beings who are responsible and caring, contributing members of our society.

For middle-school students, use Inspiration Software (Westhaver 1997); it works well for brainstorming. Encourage the students to brainstorm and create a web with each of them at the center and all their links to the community and the world. Have them describe their web on the word processor and share in class or with their electronic penpals around the world.

Here's a way to work at WORLD PEACE!

## 77. The Exercise of Power

**Procedure:** Read a book to your students such as *Yertle the Turtle and Other Stories* by Dr. Seuss (Seuss 1988). Discuss Yertle's drive to be the king of all he could see. Talk about the good and bad uses of power. Encourage students to write about experiences in their lives where power has been used for good or bad purposes.

## 78. Seeking or Avoiding Human Relationships

**Procedure:** Read a book such as *The Relatives Came* by Cynthia Rylant (Rylant 1986), in which the illustrations and text convey both the exuberance and exhaustion of a family reunion. Discuss how important family and friends are in our lives and the responsibility we have to never let them down. Have students write about a time when they really enjoyed being with a friend or family member.

##  79. Sibling Rivalry

**Procedure:** Read *The One in the Middle Is the Green Kangaroo* by Judy Blume (Blume 1992). This is a story about Freddy Dissel who feels left out being the middle kid in the family. He feels like "the peanut butter part of a sandwich," squeezed between an older brother and little sister. All your students have a place in a family and that place has a big effect on their lives. Many are not happy with their location in the family; this is a good subject to discuss.

*The Pain and the Great One* is another one of Judy Blume's books (Blume 1984) that does an excellent job on this topic. Suggest the students write about their place in the family and what is good about it and not so good about it. Have them share their computer stories with the group. As they find out that there are many common feelings amongst them, they will begin to feel better about their place in the family.

## 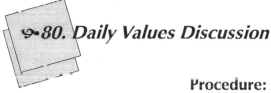 80. Daily Values Discussion

**Procedure:** Have a time each day when students can share an issue that they heard on TV or read in the paper. Write the name of the issue on the board. As students write on the computer, have them write their pro or con on the issues, print it out, and put it in a class notebook for all to read and share.

## 81. Songwriting—Writing Lyrics for Songs

**Procedure:** Music has fantastic powers for opening our minds to learning and helping us commit things to memory. Bring in the lyrics from some of the children's favorite songs. Write them on the board, encourage the children to type them on the computer and read them with the computer after they are written. Then they can print them out, and they are ready to sing with the group. Play a tune for them and encourage them to make up their own words for the song and type them on the computer. After they print out the words, they can sing them with the tune for the class.

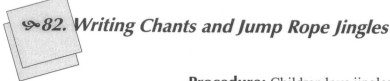

## ✒82. *Writing Chants and Jump Rope Jingles*

**Procedure:** Children love jingles and jumping rope. Visit any playground and hear such refrains as the Alphabet Jump that goes something like this:

> A—My name is Alice.
> And I come from Alabama.
> My husband's name is Al.
> And we love to eat Apples.

Let your students continue through the alphabet, writing a jingle for each letter and then playing it back on the computer for the whole class to enjoy and then join in on reading.

## ✒83. *Writing Riddles*

Who doesn't enjoy a riddle?

**What is black and white and read all over?**
**The newspaper!**

**Procedure:** You can find information and more riddles at:

http://www.squiglysplayhouse.com/JokesAnd
Riddles/index.html#Riddles

You can use the book *Alphabet Riddles* by Susan Joyce (Joyce 1998) or *Bennett Cerf's Book of Riddles* (Cerf 1989). Either of these books will delight your students with challenging riddles and give them an idea of how to make up one of their own.

After you have read lots of riddles to your students, give them time to create their own on the computer, print them out and bind them together to make "Our Class Riddle Book."

## ✒84. *Writing Jokes*

Laughter is good medicine for all of us, and humor in the classroom is important. Your children love Knock Knock jokes and enjoy reading and making up jokes.

**Procedure:** A good place to begin is *The Joke Book* by Roy McKie (McKie 1979), but you will find lots of children's joke books in your school library. Also visit the Web site in Activity #83 for jokes as well as riddles.

Have a joke of the day posted on your board. Encourage your students to print out their jokes and choose a student to compile the jokes into a book called "Our Class Joke Book."

## ✍ 85. The Great American Novel

At age five, in kindergarten, Libby started what could evolve into a great romance novel. At age six, David, a first-grader, began a twenty-six-page story that could someday blossom into a John Updike kind of novel.

**Procedure:** Encourage your students to keep working on their favorite stories that they have written daily and develop them into novels. With CD-ROM software, they can take the writing with them each year and end up with a publishable novel when they graduate from eighth grade.

A. Scott Berg, the Pulitzer Prize–winning author of the biography on Charles Lindbergh, took ten years to complete the work. Your students can be well on their way if they reside in writing, publishing classrooms like yours.

## ✍ 86. From Writing Individual Pieces to Creating Research Reports

Two skills are helpful when teaching your students to change from their daily story writing to the writing of research reports. They are creating an Idea Map and a Concept Map.

**Procedure:** Inspiration Software, www.inspiration.com, is a wonderful program to introduce to your students. In Inspiration, students think and learn visually. Remember that this generation of students you now teach has had TV and computers for their entire lives so they are very skilled at learning visually. I will not put an age minimum on the use of this software for it depends strictly on the needs and interests of each student. At age two and a half, my granddaughter Colleen skillfully completes fifty-piece puzzles and uses the computer and CD-ROM daily with ease.

As we begin to introduce report writing and longer story writing, Inspiration is a must. It has two main views or environments: Diagram View and Outline View. *You can model and teach your students the uses of diagrams, concept maps, idea maps, webbing, storyboards and outlines.* All of these provide your students with support for their visual thinking and preparation of materials for reports. As a journalist, my daughter gives her fifth-grade teacher, Alice French, credit for supporting her writing through teaching her webbing skills. You will be able to provide this kind of inspiration and support for all your students.

See the following samples for an example of the kind of work students can do. You need to provide a model that you have created for them to see and then allow them to try and develop their own.

*An Idea Map.* Students can create an idea map as illustrated in Figure 17. This is a visual brainstorming technique used to generate ideas and develop thoughts. An idea map starts with a main idea and links subideas to it. Model one for your students, then encourage them to develop their own.

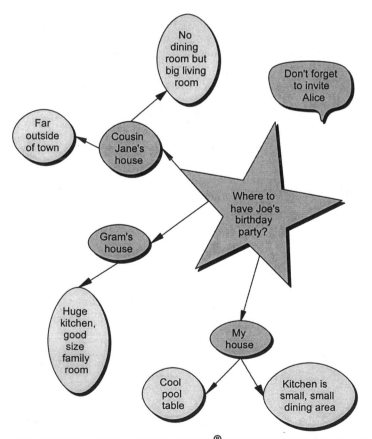

This diagram was created using Inspiration® by Inspiration Software, Inc. Used by permission.

*Figure 17. Idea Map. Copyright 1999 by Inspiration Software, Inc.*

*A Concept Map.* A concept map is a hierarchical diagram used to represent a set of concepts beginning with the most general or most important, and then working down to more specific detail. This is very useful to model for your students when teaching report writing. See Figure 18 for an example of how to begin a concept map.

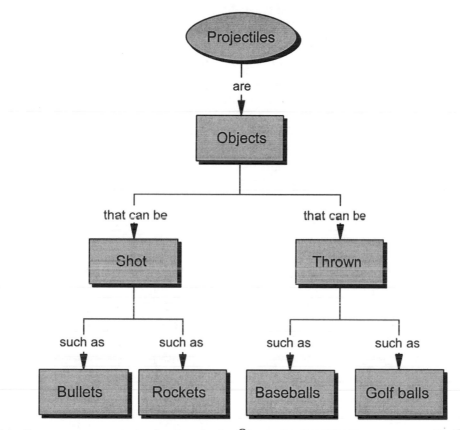

This diagram was created using Inspiration ® by Inspiration Software, Inc. Used by permission.

*Figure 18. Concept Map. Copyright 1999 by Inspiration Software, Inc.*

## ∾87. *History Comes Alive*

**Procedure:** When you ask adults what subjects they liked in school, many say, "I hated history because of memorizing all those dates and not really understanding it." Once in a while you ask someone who says, "I loved it. My teacher made it so interesting. She told us stories of the famous peoples' lives and made us understand how it felt to live at that time. It was my favorite class."

We all need to find information meaningful to really learn it, and we all love stories. You can make history come alive for your students by making it real. Share some of the exciting lives of historical characters. The books written by Jean Fritz are great examples of stories that will make history come alive for your students. Read *George Washington's Breakfast* (Fritz 1969)—it puts your students right at the breakfast table with George. *Shh! We're Writing the Constitution* (Fritz 1987) is another book by Fritz that has wonderful illustrations by Tomie dePaola—it is one you don't want to miss. Your students could even role play being signers of the Constitution after hearing that one.

Encourage your students to select a historical person they are interested in and find out all they can through classroom books and the Internet. Then they can each write the story of their character or what they think they would have done if they had been that character and lived at that time.

# ✑88. Month-to-Month Ideas

**Procedure:**  Month by Month, a new CD-ROM program with print materials by Knowledge Adventure, presents an activity kit of lessons, templates, clip art and ideas designed by teachers of Pre-K to Grade 4 to be used with KidWorks Deluxe Software. This program will give you more activities and clip art coordinated to theme-based instruction and monthly activities to use in your classroom. You can find out more information about this product on their Web site at

www.knowledgeadventure.com

Your students will develop reading, writing, math, science, social studies, and drawing and painting skills as they discover what makes each day of their year special. And they will create all kinds of books to share with friends and classmates.

January is an excellent month to make resolutions for the year. Share your New Year's resolution with your students and have them write theirs on the computer. See this excellent resource for activities like this all through the year.

# Part III

# *Your Publishing Classroom*

## Model of Classroom Design

**My first thought** was to share with you how some teacher designed her classroom, but then I realized this is what you need to do yourself based on the space you have and the needs of your children. So I will limit myself to some suggestions of what you must make sure to have in your class to make it a writing, publishing environment.

My suggestion is to set up the room in centers or areas for specific purposes. See Figure 19. Of course, a library center with plenty of comfortable places to read is a must—see if someone will donate some rocking chairs.

You also need an Author's Chair center where authors can be found reading their latest works. The Author's Chair is a way to showcase the child's writing accomplishments. The children can sign up to read their own writing, the writing of a classmate or a trade book. After the reading, the author answers questions and responds to classmates' reactions to the story.

You need to have the following:

- a computer center with at least six networked computers where budding writers are writing across the curriculum all day long

- U-shaped coaching table for you to conference with children on their writings and give them feedback and suggestions

- an editing section with baseball caps labeled *Editor* where lots of peer conferencing, collaboration on stories and editing takes place

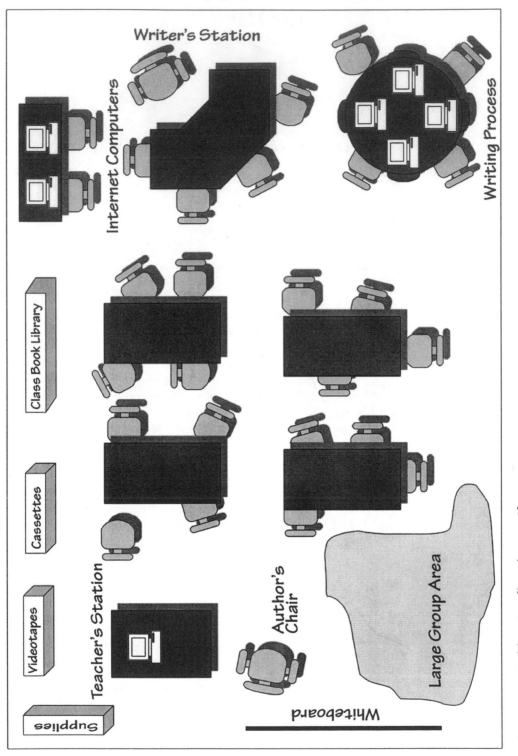

*Figure 19. A Writing, Reading Literacy Classroom*

- a telecommunications center where at least one computer is hooked up to an online service and students communicate daily with their counterparts elsewhere in the world

- a presentation station where, using HyperStudio, groups of children can develop plays, stories, reports and presentations and then, using the projection monitor, share them with the entire class. (This can be the same as the teacher's station in the front of the class.)

- an Internet station with computers that are hooked up to the Internet for global penpal communications.

If you have that much, don't forget your own computer on your desk with an LCD projection monitor so you can daily make presentations, share your writing and edit your own work for students to witness the thinking that occurs when a writer edits her own work. You will find your computer to be invaluable for writing frequent parent notes, communicating with colleagues online for the latest information and support in your teaching and also to make easier the record-keeping chores that come with the job of teacher.

One of the most important things a teacher can bring to the classroom is the model of the teacher as a reader, writer, speaker, lover of literature and user of technology. Always remember that your students want to be like you and other successful adults that they see. Children will be motivated to use the computer whether you do or not, but they will be much more likely to use the computer as a practical, integrated tool for learning if they see a teacher doing the same. Use the computer during whole and small group instruction and for recording class stories and producing class signs and charts.

## The Author's Chair

Having our work heard by an audience is a very important part of authorship. Have a special chair in the front of the room selected and labeled as The Author's Chair. A canvas director's chair on which you have printed *Author* on the canvas will work very well. Children and the teacher sit in this chair and read the books that they have written to the class. This is the only time anyone sits in this chair. Teachers at all grade levels use an Author's Chair.

When teachers sit in the chair to read books aloud to students, they model the technique by naming the author, the illustrator and sharing something about the book. When teachers show a book they have written, they explain something about why they wrote it before they read it. Students learn to do the same kind of presentation when they are the author and have the privilege of sitting in this special chair—introducing the book they wrote, explaining why they wrote it and then reading it to their peers.

You need to help your children understand what are good questions, appropriate comments and compliments to share with an author. Give them some examples before the first author takes his place.

*An added benefit of the Author's Chair is a place where the teacher sits when she reads to the class daily. It is a place to discuss books and the important role that writing and reading plays in our lives.*

# The Teacher's Role in the Writing Process

When Shelley Harwayne, co-director of the Teachers College Writing Project, drew a chair alongside Ipolito Diaz's desk, the boy sighed deeply. "I don't have anything to write about," he said. "All I do is watch TV, feed the pigeons, watch TV, feed the pigeons." "Is one of those topics especially important?" Shelley asked. "Well," Ipolito answered, "I suppose feeding the pigeons is more important because if I don't feed them, they'll starve." When Shelley suggested that Ipolito write on the topic, he looked dubious. "It'll be awful short," he answered, and to illustrate his point, Ipolito recited the story: "I-feed-pigeons."

Undaunted, Shelly encouraged him to observe everything the next time he fed the pigeons. Several weeks later, he stood before his class and read what he had written:

> Boo, Coo a soft whisper
> Calls me to the yard
> Grey, silver birds
> Greeting me
> Crowding me, watching me, pecking at my feet.
> Piles of yellow, minute, hard corn
> Stampedes of homers, flights, tiplits, maggies,
> Rollers, turbans, owls swooping and charging.
> Pecking, pushing, struggling
> Done!
> The same scramble for a drink
> Full and lazy
> Time to sleep
> Goodnight pigeons.

Shelley's model demonstrates beautifully the role you have in the classroom: to listen, to encourage and to inspire students to write about what is meaningful to them.

Here are helpful strategies to use when students are writing with computers.

1.   Be friendly, patient, encouraging.

2.   Sit at the student's eye level.

3. Encourage the child to spell words the way they sound.

4. Keep the focus on the flow of ideas; ask leading questions.

5. Ask questions to extend stories.

6. Give specific praise.

7. Provide opportunities to read and share stories.

8. Provide guidance in hearing phonemes.

9. Help edit for phonemic consistency.

10. Avoid writing as "copying."

11. Guide self-editing.

12. Accept quiet talking.

13. Provide multiple materials and orderly storage.

14. Value students' writing by posting and publishing their works.

15. Extend "coaching staff" with volunteers, older students, peers.

Despite the enormous advances in computing, technology remains a tool—a powerful tool to write with, think with, explore ideas with—but nevertheless a tool, a sophisticated pencil. It can never be the substitute for the personal touch of the classroom teacher; in fact, even more skilled teachers are need to model, facilitate, coach and instruct students in this new medium. How teachers implement computers in the schools is critical, for without proper integration of computers into the curriculum, the benefits of technology use for children will not be attained.

# Evaluation of Writing Pieces and Projects

### 1. Self-Evaluation of Writing by Students
One of the most effective evaluation tools we have is self-evaluation or reflection on what we have written. For every activity and writing the students do on the talking computer, have them listen to the computer read it back to them and make a determination of its effectiveness themselves first. Is this what I wanted to say? How can I change it to make it better?

### 2. Peer Evaluation
Peers, if they are coached about how to help a writer, can offer valuable suggestions.

### 3. Holistic Evaluation of Writing by Teachers
Using a holistic writing evaluation guide, teachers can make an objective decision as to the level of quality of the work, although you as a teacher will also know the specific circumstances involved in

each student's productions and that will help you make a fair assessment. See the chart below.

---

## ❧ *Criteria for Scoring Writing Samples* ❧

### Level Explanation

6      Ideas are very well developed and expressed. The writing has a fully developed structure, which may or may not be narrative. The ideas are connected logically and they are well organized. There is good sentence variety and expression.

5      Ideas are fairly well developed and expressed. The writing has a discernible structure. The ideas are connected logically, but they are not so fully developed or so well organized as score 6 papers.

4      Ideas are only loosly connected or not developed. The structure may be disjointed, but what is provided is clearly more than a list. The ideas are relevant but are not developed or expressed well. The sentence structure may be repetitious.

3      Ideas lack development. The writing often merely lists ideas. The phrasing and the sentence structure are repetitious.

2      Ideas have little or no relationship to a topic. An idea or a list is provided. Minimal paper.

1      Only letters or unrelated simple words. All that is presented is a copy of a prompt, or words or phrases the child sees displayed in the room.

PW      Prewriting, or mock writing

---

*4. Portfolio Evaluation of Writing by Student, Teacher, Parents*

Students should be writing daily and saving their work in a portfolio. Several times a year before parent conferencing, select a sample of the writings with each child. Evaluate these samples according to Writing Stage.

### *Stages of Writing*

- Stage 1—*Early Writing*
  The students experiment with letters, capital and lowercase. They write their names, some letters, names of family members. There's no spacing; letters are mixed with numbers. Symbols and punctuation marks from the computer keyboard are randomly printed.

- Stage 2—*Simple Phrases or Sentences*
  The students are beginning to create three or more word phrases or sentences. They copy words from the print environment in the room on the computer.

- Stage 3—*Simple Story*
  Students create a simple story but it has a point to it, or a beginning and an end.

- Stage 4—*Stories*
  The students are beginning to use descriptive words and write much longer stories.

- Stage 5—*Long Stories*
  Students can write stories in many genres. They are beginning to use book spelling, descriptive words, complex sentences, dialogue and punctuation.

To illustrate to you how important your students' daily writing is as an authentic assessment tool for you, look at the following three samples.

First is Shaun's writing and picture (see Figure 20). Can you read what he wrote? Here's a clue—he's an avid Star Wars fan. Any luck yet? Well, you guessed correctly if you thought it says:

<u>"Return of the Jedi."</u>

Now, as the teacher, ask, What skills does Shaun still need? Well the first one is obvious: spaces between words. Will you mark up his writing with red marks? Of course not. The best way to point out the spaces authors use between words is to use a Star Wars book you have in class, point out to him how the spaces between words make it easier to read and the next time he writes, he should try that.

*Figure 20. Shaun's Work*

The next sample is Brandon's work, a first-grader in an inner city school (see Figure 21). If you looked at his drawing alone and made an assessment about his developmental level according to a Gesell Developmental Scale, what would you guess? Most teachers say three or four years of age, which would put him in a really low first-grade group. However, now look at the top of the page. Brandon typed this before he even illustrated it with his drawing. Look closely, does he have phonemic awareness? Yes, how about punctuation and sentence structure? Yes, and how about the sense of story? Of course, he is a very bright first-grade boy, and in the past we would have mis-labeled and misjudged his intelligence based on his motor skill, which is still undeveloped. Think of all the mistakes we made calling students "low level" or "learning disabled" just because we did not have the computer as a tool for them to write with and demonstrate to us the ideas they really had.

*Figure 21. Brandon's Story*

Anthony is a third-grader and he wrote a story with a pencil and then typed one on the same day (see Figure 22). Can you see the difference in his ability when given the computer to write with? It demonstrates why we need at least six networked computers in every classroom, if not one per child, to support their daily writing and empower their literacy development.

Anthony

One day my friend and I couldn't wait to go trick or treat in my city. We couldn't wait to go but 1 more day was Halloween. It was Halloween and we went to my first neighbor and my mom, dad, my friend and I saw a real monster at our first neighbor's house. We saw it go into this scary place that nobody went to before. Then we went into the haunted house it was very scary. The monster looked very scary then he was attacking my family and my friend. Then we got our fake weapons, my mom and my dad were using a water gun. My sister and my other sister was using a hammer, my friend and I was using a stick. Then we fought the monster and my mom shot water in the monster's eyes. My sister hit the monster's foot with the hammer. My friend and I was using the stick to hit the monster's stomache. Then he died and we went home.

The End!

*Figure 22. Anthony's Story*

# Editing: The Important Step
# Before Publication

If you have a class rule that everyone reads what they have written to at least three people in the class, you will find that as they re-read what they have written, they very naturally begin to edit their work. Orlando was a five-year-old Downs Syndrome, limited English speaker when he wrote the following page (see Figure 23) on the computer. He went to his seat, re-read his work and noticed that when he copied the word *yellow* from a list on the board, he left out the W. Notice how he edited his own work by adding the W with his pencil. If Orlando could do this at age five, all of your students are capable of editing their own work. You must convey your confidence in them and also model good editing techniques to them.

**Procedure:** The first step is for you as the teacher to model the editing process. Select a story you have written that has punctuation, capitalization and spacing errors. Show it on the overhead projector and do editing of your work for all the students to see. Introduce them to proofreading, using the following editing marks.

Demonstrate how you use these marks as you proofread your work for all of the class. Then have them choose one of their favorite writings from their portfolio and work with a partner and use the proofreaders' chart to correct their work. You will walk around the class wearing a baseball cap with *Editor* on the front of it and offer assistance. Talk about how they can help one another be peer editors of their work. Remind them that all work must be edited before it can be published into a book.

---

## ❧ *Proofreaders' Chart* ❧

| | |
|---|---|
| Insert ∧ | A baby cat is ∧a kitten. *(called, inserted above)* |
| Capitalize ≡ | cats love to chase after mice. |
| Change to lower case / | Why do Cats sleep during the day? |
| Add period ⊙ | Cats and dogs can get along together. |
| Add comma ∧ | Some cats dogs birds are in the zoo. |
| Delete ℮ | Many cats are tiny and little creatures. |
| Add apostrophe ∨ | People love to buy cats toys. |

Orlando
cat dog dog  fish pig
The pig The pig The pig
red blue greenblack
yello

*Figure 23. Orlando's Work*

Another suggestion is to have cross-age tutors or students from higher grades come to your class during editing time. Having an editing corner in your classroom is helpful; you can have several *Editor* baseball caps there available for students to use when they are editing work.

You can create an Editing Checklist for students to use when they are doing peer editing.

---

*Editing Checklist for Our Class*

Work done by    _____    Author

                      _____    Editor

_____ 1. I have checked that all sentences begin with capital letters.

_____ 2. I have checked the spelling of all words and circled misspellings.

_____ 3. I have checked that all sentences end with punctuation marks.

_____ 4. I have checked that all proper nouns begin with capital letters.

_____ 5. I have inserted missing words.

---

# Publishing: The Final Step

Your students have been writing daily in your classroom. Now is the time for them to evaluate what they have written; this is their responsibility. After they have completed about four stories, have them select the best one. You should do the same, then discuss with them the choices you both have made. They need to defend the strengths of the work they feel should be published.

Your role in helping your students become storywriters is:

1. Be a storyteller and storywriter yourself; share your own personal stories orally and in print on the computer for them daily. Your role model and inspiration is most important.

2. Listen to the stories they tell and provide them with the computer tools to put their words in print early in the year to prove to them they are writers.

3. Expect them all to have stories and provide opportunities for them to tell their stories and create audiences for those stories.

4. Model good responses and hold individual and group writing conferences regularly to give them practice in giving and receiving responses.

5. Show them how to publish their writing on the computer to validate it as a body of literature and to make it available as a resource.

6. Invite children's authors into your classroom or school to share with the children how they write and publish their stories.

# Book Binding

There are many ways to create books for your classroom library. KidWorks Deluxe prints out students' writing in a small four-page fold-up book or large 8½ x 11 pages to be bound together as books (see sample book on pages 98 99). Students should add an All About the Author page at the back of their books, just like the page that published books have with a picture and some information about the author.

Students can construct booklets by stapling the pages together or using a three-hole punch on pages and putting them in binders; this works well for books that contain all the class work.

Students can use cardboard covers, covered with wallpaper, contact paper or cloth.

# Classroom Library

Designate a special corner of your classroom to have the books created by your class on display. Students should have library time to read and enjoy the works that they have written as well as those written by their peers. Have a cassette tape or video camera available and record or film authors as they read their own books in the Author's Chair. You can have these cassettes and videos available in the library for the students to view as well.

One of the most powerful ways we learn is from one another. Have some videos of well-known authors who have written books your students really enjoy available for them to view. Also remember to invite published authors to your classroom to talk to your students whenever you have that opportunity. Contact your local library to find out when various authors might be available.

As you present works from favorite authors to your students, encourage them to write a letter to the author, expressing how they enjoyed the book. These letters can be sent in care of the publisher whose address is in the front pages of the book. Another good activity is to have each of your students pick a favorite author and then present books by that author to the entire class.

# A Learning Revolution

One of the most exciting discoveries you will make as you use these activities daily in your classroom is how much your students each have to contribute. You will be constantly amazed at their ideas and the development of their own voice in writing. You will realize that the heart of good education is learner-centered. When the students have an interest and the need to know and are given a new tool to support their writing, they will be successful authors, readers and well on their way to being lifelong learners. You will never want to return to the old ways. Students who in the past felt like failures now will be some of your most productive writers. You as an educator now see with new eyes the desire to learn and be successful that resides in each one of us.

You will find that you write more yourself, and may be considering writing the next novel on a "Day in the Life of a Teacher." We need teachers who are readers and read stories of their own interest during uninterrupted silent, sustained reading time when students are reading books of their interest and choice. Teachers and parents who are avid lifelong learners will transfer this desire to students. For you see, the students want to be like us. They don't want to do drill and kill and be kept busy; they don't want to be labeled and put in a box; they don't want to be treated like empty vessels needing to be filled up with testing information. They learn like you and I do—when they are interested and have a need to know.

We all have a great universal human need to know. The computer and the ability it gives us to reflect on the information resident in our brains as well as accessing the information that is resident in the billions of other brains on our earth can open up a learning revolution like we have never known. Perhaps what you have learned most from your students' daily writings is the immense power the human brain has to learn and to grow when given the right tools and environment and allowed to pursue its own path. There are many ways that the teacher can integrate technology into her classroom to make her job easier, to empower the writing of all of her students, to enrich her curriculum and to bring to her classroom the resources of the world. The time to start is *now* so that every child has a chance for literacy success and also access to the information needed as a citizen of the twenty-first century.

Part **IV**

# Home School Connection: How Can a Parent Provide a Good Written Language Environment at Home?

*Note to teachers: Replicate this section on parent support for computers in the home and school and present to parents at an open house, or send home with parents.*

**Parents will ask** you what kinds of things they should have their children doing on a computer. You can recommend to them the book *Young Kids and Computers: A Parent's Survival Guide* by Children's Software Revue (Children's Software Revue, 44 Main St., Flemington, NJ 08822, 1-800-993-9499). Information on the book can be found at www.childrenssoftware.com. You might also want to copy the following information and checklist of ideas to include in one of your parent newsletters.

## What Parents Need to Know About Computers for Their Young Children

As the number of computers in homes dramatically increases, the small child's interest in computers is rapidly spreading. One of my student teachers reported to me that when she comes home and works on her computer, her two-year-old looks at her and says, "When is my puter time, Mommy?"

93

Children are very empowered by learning the letters of the alphabet easily on the keyboard. The computer allows them to make the letters and then hear them spoken so they are learning the alphabet and having fun at the same time. Programs such as KidWorks Deluxe or Writing Blaster that are talking word processing programs with graphic capabilities allow children to write any letters or words they want and hear them spoken back for them to read along with, then they can print them out. The graphic program allows children to create drawings and talk about these creations to you, thus expanding their oral language development and fostering their development of storytelling. The word boxes in KidWorks Deluxe present many common words and pictures that children can select and put in their stories. These pictures can be used for rebus stories (stories in which we substitute a picture for a word) and are very motivating to children and helpful for vocabulary development. KidPix is another fine program that allows the child to be in control of his learning and to create writings and drawings of his own.

Scollon and Scollon found that when their four-year-old son first had the opportunity to use a word processor, his experimentation was similar to what his sister had done by hand. He typed nonsense characters first, but then he began to type communications. They maintain that the word processor made it easier for him to generate legible messages. Many children have experiences similar to this because their parents use computers at home for work (Scollon and Scollon 1984).

Another kind of software really appropriate for early childhood is the Broderbund Living Books Series. These Interactive Animated Stories for children are just that, interactive, so the child has a great deal of control in choosing what actions to view. The child can hear favorite children's literature read in English, Spanish or Japanese. The words are highlighted as they are read so children can make sound-word connections and subliminally pick up left to right directionality. Hearing the stories again and again helps develop a sense of story, rhythm of language and love of reading. My grandson Will at age two and a half mastered use of the mouse after a simple five-minute demonstration by me and enjoyed the story "Ruff's Bone" again and again. Two- and three-year-olds can start the computer, find their program, boot the disk and do other amazing things. The human brain is at its peak in the early years, ready to absorb many languages. The computer is a language that children take to as easily as they take to their native language or the second language a parent or caregiver speaks to them during these early years.

*One caution for parents:* When selecting software for your child, keep one guideline in the back of your mind. Select only software that is a tool for your child to write, draw, calculate and learn with; or software that is interactive and your child can select information according to her interests; or software that is an information resource such as encyclopedias. Avoid drill programs that are glorified worksheets that promise to drill your child on phonics, math facts or any number of other lessons. Avoid game programs that have little educational value.

Parents eager for more information about using computers with children should read Seymour Papert's book *The Children's Machine* (Papert 1993) or his other book *The Connected Family* (Papert 1996). Join the Computer Using Educator group in your community and access the World Wide Web sites that have reviews of children's software. You can also use online resources such as America Online and Compu-Serve to get information for parents on children and computers.

# Using KidWorks Deluxe or a Talking Word Processor with Your Child

Allow your children time to just teach themselves letters on the keyboard. They like to type different letters and hear them spoken. They like to explore language so they will type names they know and type words that they see in print around the room, then they love to hear them spoken. Just like adults do but hate to confess, children often type funny or "bad" words on the computer to hear how they sound; in all cases they are learning about language. Let them explore the graphic program and create pictures that they would like to have in a story. Giving them simple encouragement and praise for what they are writing are what you need to do. If they write, "I have a new friend," ask them to read it to you and then nudge a little, "What is the friend's name, and what does he like to do?" After the child prints out the story, have her read it to you and display it proudly on the refrigerator. Accept spelling that conveys the message to you even if it is not yet proper English spelling. Remember that you didn't start spelling perfectly either; this will come for them as they listen to you read or read along with you daily and notice the book spelling in the books they see.

Be proud of your child's creations and don't forget to share them with Grandma and Grandpa, who will also appreciate them.

# Checklist for Parents

Remember that:

1.  Children use the sounds they hear to help them write their own speech; it is not unusual for them to write *wuz* for *was* or *skool* for *school*—this is just a stage in their writing development. Remember how their first words were incomplete, *ba ba* for *bottle*, and you showed you understood and got excited about your child's first words. Well, the same thing is essential for their beginning writing; don't mark up their words or correct them and make them do it over. Let them read it to you and be pleased about their

message. When you write them a note, use conventional spelling; they will see teachers doing this and see the book spelling in all they read and before you know it, they will be using it.

2.   Children all work at their own pace; do not compare this child with your other children.

3.   Read to your child daily, and visit the library often.

4.   Read and memorize poems, jingles and songs together. Music has great power in helping us learn and remember. Also read and share jokes and funny stories; children love to laugh, and it's good for you too. Remember learning does not have to be painful; in fact, it can be fun!

5.   Provide many writing materials for your child: word processor or typewriter, different kinds of pens, pencils, crayons, markers, chalk and papers.

6.   Help your child notice and write words and letters she sees on boxes, labels, signs, etc.

7.   Listen to your child read what he has written. Remember if he can read it, he is an author already.

8.   Display your child's work. Try the refrigerator as a special place for all to see it.

9.   Share in your child's joy of learning. It's the strongest reward you can give! Try not to criticize. Hug your child and tell her you love her every day; we all need to hear that.

10.  Write your child notes in his lunch box, under his pillow, or as a fun treasure hunt around the house.

11.  Encourage your child to write notes and lists: wish lists, shopping lists, letters to relatives, thank-you notes, notes to the teacher and friends. Get your child an online or mail penpal to write to in another country.

## *Completing the Author's Place*

Research shows that children who are not read to at home and do not get appropriate early experiences arrive at school three thousand hours behind those who have had the appropriate help at home. By sending the previous section to your parents, you are helping them understand the best ways they can contribute to their child's developing literacy. Now you have informed parents about the learning going on in your Author's Place classroom and given them suggestions on how to support their child's writing and reading at home; this home support and transfer of knowledge is essential to the success of any literacy program.

You have learned to be the coach, encourager, diagnostician and advocate for each of your students. You have written, sung, read and enjoyed the benefits of literacy with them. You have shown them the excitement of being a lifelong learner. Now you are the expert on what works in using technology to empower learners, and armed with this knowledge, you can create many other wonderful ideas of your own for your students. Remember that you now have the fantastic resources of the Internet, and lesson ideas can be found there at your fingertips. Also visit our Author's Place Web page at www.lu.com/lu/kidsauthors/ for updates on ideas and suggestions about the latest software. After all, you are the only one who really knows the interest and skill needs of your students. It is your responsibility to select appropriate materials and when you find the right material, and you say the right words of encouragement, all of a sudden, one of your students will light up and say, "I can read, thank you, teacher!"

The late John Henry Martin, educator and author of *Writing to Read*, summed up your reward well when he said:

> The computer can give the learner the world's most beautiful feeling, the Greek "Eureka": I got it, I know it, I can see it, I can understand it! That's a transforming feeling; to be awakened from dormancy, from sadness to strength, to dignity. I can write, I can read!
> —Dr. John Henry Martin

Give this gift to each of your students.

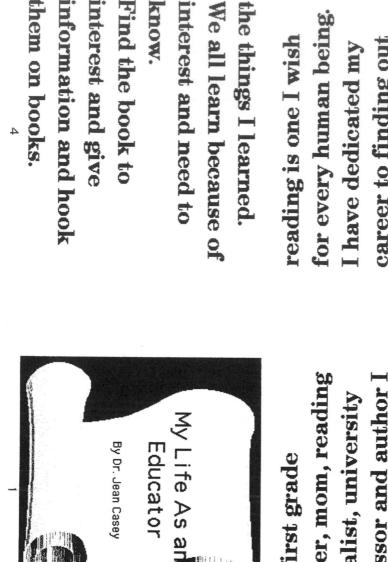

My Life As an Educator

By Dr. Jean Casey

1

As a first grade teacher, mom, reading specialist, university professor and author I have always been in awe of the moment when a child says, I can read! The gift of

2

reading is one I wish for every human being. I have dedicated my career to finding out how to best help each person achieve this wonderful life goal. This book has some of

3

the things I learned. We all learn because of interest and need to know.

Find the book to interest and give information and hook them on books.

4

We all need to be successful so provide a tool and encouragement where the person can write and read the first day they try. This is the talking word processor.

5

When you select a talking word processor make sure it has: fix speech where you can adjust the pronunciation of words.

6

With the graphic features all your students can fly like eagles and be successful in creating their very own books!

7

They can write about their world.

8

Here is the list of software suggested throughout this activity book. You can use any word processing program that you have, but remember that the talking feature really enhances the learning for many students, and I recommend that.

KidWorks Deluxe is an excellent talking word processing program to support all these activities. Month by Month for KidWorks Deluxe contains theme-based writing projects for every month of the year. These ideas, available on CD-ROM, will be a valuable addition to your classroom. They are accessories for the Kid-Works Deluxe program. It provides additional ideas on how your students will love expressing themselves through words, pictures and a host of activities. Students can create their own books, which you save as "player files" that can be sent home and shared with family and friends. KidWorks Deluxe is published by Knowledge Adventure, 1-800-545-7677, ext. 1239, e-mail: SchoolSales@KnowledgeAdventure.com

HyperStudio by Roger Wagner is another excellent classroom writing and publishing program. It allows your students to create multimedia presentations combining graphics, text, music and design. It is also available from Knowledge Adventure, 1-800-545-7677, hyperstudio@education.com

Inspiration Software is an excellent program for middle- and upper-grade study skills such as webbing, mapping, and organizing thought. It is from Inspiration Software Inc., 1-800-877-4292, ext. 30. www.inspiration.com

Waterford Early Reading Program is the latest early literacy total reading program that I have reviewed that outdoes all its predecessors. It has outstanding meaningful content, beautiful graphics, fine music and a talking word processor as well. I am sure that it will be the next best program to be a part of the writing, publishing literacy classroom. It is developed by Waterford Institute, Sandy, Utah, published and distributed by Electronic Education, Sunnyvale, CA, 1-888-977-7900, derrin.hill@electroniceducation.com

KidPix is a good word processing program and the Living Books Series has excellent interactive children's books on CD-ROMs. From Broderbund Software, a division of the Learning Company.

The Ultimate Writing and Creativity Center is an excellent talking word processor for grades four and up. These products are available through the Learning Company at 1-800-685-6322.

For more information on the theory of language processing, the history of the language machine and research results from around the world that prove the effectiveness of the computer in the early classroom, refer to the revised edition of *Early Literacy: The Empowerment of Technology* by Jean M. Casey (Libraries Unlimited 2000).

# References

AGC Educational Media. (1999). ABC Animals. Evanston, IL, AGC Educational Media.

Ahlberg, J., and A. Ahlberg. (1986). *Jolly Postman*. New York, Little Brown & Co.

Barrett, J. (1982). *Cloudy with a Chance of Meatballs*. New York, Aladdin.

Base, G. (1983). *Animalia*. New York, Harry N. Abrams.

Blume, J. (1984). *The Pain and the Great One*. New York, Simon & Schuster.

———. (1992). *The One in the Middle Is the Green Kangaroo*. New York, Dell.

Broderbund. (1999). Where in the World Is Carmen San Diego? Novato, CA, Broderbund.

Brown, M. W. (1974). *The Runaway Bunny*. New York, HarperCollins.

Casey, J. M. (2000). *Early Literacy: The Empowerment of Technology*, rev. ed. Englewood, CO, Libraries Unlimited.

Cerf, B. (1989). *Bennett Cerf's Book of Riddles*. New York, Random House.

Charney, R. S. (1992). *Teaching Children to Care*. Boston, Northeast Foundation for Children.

Chomsky, C. (1978). "When You Still Can't Read in Third Grade: After Decoding, What?" In: *What Research Has to Say About Reading Instruction*, ed. S. J. Samuels. Newark, DE, International Reading Association.

Cleary, B. (1984). *Dear Mr. Henshaw*. New York, William Morrow & Co.

Clinton, H. (1998). *Dear Socks, Dear Buddy*. New York, Simon & Schuster.

Coerr, E. (1999). *Sadako and the Thousand Paper Cranes*. New York, Puffin Books.

dePaola, T. (1978). *The Popcorn Book*. New York, Holiday House.

Eliot, T. S. (1984). *Old Possum's Book of Practical Cats*. San Diego, CA, Harcourt Brace.

Fritz, J. (1969). *George Washington's Breakfast*. New York, Coward-McCann.

———. (1987). *Shh! We're Writing the Constitution*. New York, Putnam.

Hutchins, P. (1983). *Rosie's Walk*. New York, Aladdin.

Joyce, S. (1998). *Alphabet Riddles*. New York, Peel.

Karelitz, E. B. (1993). *The Author's Chair*. Exeter, NH, Heinemann.

Keats, E. J. (1998). *Peter's Chair*. New York, Viking.

Kellogg, S. (1984). *Paul Bunyon*. New York, Mulberry Books.

Knowledge Adventure. (1999a). KidPhonics. Torrance, CA, Knowledge Adventure.

———. (1999b). KidWorks Deluxe. Torrance, CA, Knowledge Adventure.

Kohn, A. (1998). *What to Look for in a Classroom*. San Francisco, Jossey-Bass.

Krakauer, J. (1997). *Into Thin Air*. New York, Villard Books.

Lathrop, Ann. (1995). "California Instructional Technology Clearinghouse." Modesto, CA, Stanislaus County Office of Education.

Learning Company. (1998). The Ultimate Writing and Creativity Center. Cambridge, MA, Learning Company.

———. (1999). KidPix. Cambridge, MA, Learning Company.

Lobel, A. (1970). *Frog and Toad Are Friends*. New York, HarperCollins.

Lomask, M. (1992). *Great Lives: Invention and Technology*. New York, Atheneum.

Marcus, S. (1999). "Childhood's End?" *CUE Newsletter*, vol. 21 (May/June).

McKie, R. (1979). *The Joke Book*. New York, Random House.

Mochizuki, K. (1993). *Baseball Saved Us*. New York, Lee & Low.

Papert, S. (1993). *The Children's Machine*. New York, Basic Books.

———. (1996). *The Connected Family: Bridging the Generation Gap*. Atlanta, GA, Longstreet Press.

Parish, P. (1992). *Amelia Bedelia*. New York, HarperCollins.

Rey, H. A. (1973). *Curious George*. Boston, Houghton Mifflin.

Rowling, J. K. (1998). *Harry Potter and the Sorcerer's Stone*. London, Arthur A. Levine.

Rylant, C. (1986). *The Relatives Came*. New York, Simon & Schuster.

Scieszka, J. (1989). *The True Story of the Three Little Pigs*. New York, Viking.

———. (1992). *The Stinky Cheese Man and Other Fairly Stupid Tales*. New York, Viking.

Scollon, S. B., and R. Scollon. (1984). "Run Trilogy: Can Tommy Read?" In: *Awakening to Literacy*, ed. H. Goelman, A. Oberg, and F. Smith. Exeter, NH, Heinemann.

Seuss, Dr. (1988). *Yertle the Turtle and Other Stories*. New York, Random House.

———. (1998). *The Lorax*. New York, Random House.

Shaw, N. (1988). *Sheep in a Jeep*. Boston, Houghton Mifflin.

Silverstein, S. (1974). *Where the Sidewalk Ends*. New York, Harper & Row.

Silvey, A. (1995). *Children's Books and Their Creators*. Boston, Houghton Mifflin.

Smith, F. (1984). *The Promise and the Threat of Microcomputers in Language Education.* Victoria, BC, Able Press.

Stillman, P. R. (1989). *Families Writing.* Cincinnati, OH, Writer's Digest Books.

Stine, R. L. (1997). *Cry of the Cat, Goosebumps 2000 Series.* New York, Scholastic.

Taylor, T. (1969). *The Cay.* Garden City, NY, Doubleday.

Tell, C. (1999). "Renewing the Profession of Teaching: A Conversation with John Goodlad." *Educational Leadership*, vol. 56 (May): pp. 14–19.

Thayer, E. L. (1988). *Casey at the Bat.* Boston, David R. Godine.

Tolkien, J. R. R. (1977). *The Hobbit.* Boston, Houghton Mifflin.

Van Allsburg, C. (1987). *The Z Was Zapped.* Boston, Houghton Mifflin.

Viorst, J. (1972). *Alexander and the Terrible, Horrible, No Good, Very Bad Day.* New York, Atheneum.

———. (1981). *If I Were in Charge of the World.* New York, Atheneum Books.

———. (1993). *Earrings.* New York, Aladdin.

Warner, G. C. (1942). *The Boxcar Children.* Chicago, Albert Whitman.

Waterford Institute. (1990). The Waterford Early Reading Program. Sandy, UT, Waterford Institute.

Westhaver, D. H. (1997). Inspiration. Portland, OR, Inspiration Software.

White, E. B. (1999). *Charlotte's Web.* New York, HarperCollins.

Wiesner, D. (1999). *Tuesday.* New York, Clarion.

Yashima, T. (1955). *Crow Boy.* New York, Viking.

# Index

## About the Author

Jean M. Casey is a professor of education at California State University, Long Beach. For the last twenty-five years she has focused on the preparation of teachers. She started her career as a first-grade teacher, then became a reading specialist, a resource teacher, a software developer, a researcher and finally, a teacher educator. Her quest has always been to find the ways to support literacy for all children. She has been the pioneer researcher in the United States for using talking computers with primary-age children.

Her first book, *Early Literacy: The Empowerment of Technology*, reports her seventeen years of research and work with students, and offers her conclusions about how technology can empower the early literacy of children. She has worked with thousands of young students and is convinced that they are much brighter than we ever imagined.

Her areas of university teaching include reading, language arts, technology and social studies; currently she is a Learning Support Faculty in CalstateTEACH, an innovative new integrated teacher education program. Casey is a featured technology speaker at the International Reading Association Conference and has presented nationally and globally at conferences and workshops.

In 1999, she was named a Chancellors Distinguished Teacher Education Scholar for developing curriculum for CalStateTEACH. She has a Ph.D. in curriculum and instruction, educational technology and linguistics from the University of Southern California.

# LIBRARIES UNLIMITED

**LITERACY AND TECHNOLOGY**

**EARLY LITERACY: The Empowerment of Technology,** Revised Edition
*Jean M. Casey*

The book that inspired *Creating the Early Literacy Classroom*, this revised edition of Casey's critically acclaimed work includes important new data on how computers make a difference in advancing literacy. **Grades K–8.**
*xiv, 198p. 7x10 paper ISBN 1-56308-865-7*

**THE POWER OF READING: Insights from the Research**
*Stephen Krashen*

In this landmark work, Krashen argues that free voluntary reading is the most effective tool available for increasing a child's ability to read, write, spell, and comprehend. The results of studies and anecdotal evidence are both used effectively to promote student freedom of choice when it comes to selecting reading material. **All Levels.**
*x, 119p. 6x9 paper ISBN 1-56308-006-0*

**BRIDGES TO READING, K–3 AND 3–6: Teaching Reading Skills with Children's Literature**
*Suzanne I. Barchers*

Use quality children's literature to teach traditional reading skills! Providing a balance between traditional and literature-based instruction, these books include stimulating and instructive lessons based on approximately 150 skills commonly found in basal readers. **Grades K–3** and **3–6.**
*Grades K–3: ix, 201p. 8½x11 paper ISBN 1-56308-758-8*
*Grades 3–6: vii, 179p. 8½x11 paper ISBN 1-56308-759-6*

**TECHNOLOGY ACROSS THE CURRICULUM: Activities and Ideas**
*Marilyn J. Bazeli and James L. Heintz*

Link literature to technology with these 75 classroom-tested, ready-to-use activities. Simple instructions and reproducible activity sheets are included. **Grades 1–12.**
*x, 207p. 8½x11 paper ISBN 1-56308-444-9*

**WADING THE WORLD WIDE WEB: Internet Activities for Beginners**
*Keith Kyker*

Give students confidence-building, entry-level Internet experience, to encourage them to fully explore Web pages. **Grades 3 and up.**
*xvii, 170p. 8½x11 paper ISBN 1-56308-605-0*

## LIBRARIES UNLIMITED, INC.

88 Post Road West • P.O. Box 5007 • Westport • CT 06881
Phone: 800-225-5800 • Fax: 203-750-9790
Web site: www.lu.com